Rails to
Port and Starboard

by

John W. Gahan

Cover Design: ERIC MONKS

First published 1992 by Countyvise Limited, 1 & 3 Grove Road, Rock Ferry, Birkenhead, Wirral, Merseyside L42 3XS.

Copyright © John W. Gahan, 1992.

Photoset and printed by Birkenhead Press Limited, 1 & 3 Grove Road, Rock Ferry, Birkenhead, Merseyside L42 3XS.

ISBN 0 907768 49 0.

ACKNOWLEDGEMENTS

My grateful thanks are tendered to the following friends for assistance in the preparation of this book: Patricia Barnes for typing the original draft; Jim Peden for reading the manuscript and checking the locomotive details; Anita Glynn and Paul Raymond of the Archives Department of National Museums and Galleries on Merseyside who, over many weeks, unearthed old maps and heavy record books from the comprehensive Dock Board archive for my interested perusal. Sir James Picton's "Memorials of Liverpool", published in the 1870's was also a useful source of reference.

Illustrations:

My thanks to the following persons for the loan of photographs:

A.J. Cooper
J. Corkill
F. Dean
J. Feild
A. Fisher
The late N.N. Forbes
M. Jenkins
F. Jones
S.G. Jones
The late R.B. Parr
J.A. Peden
E.V. Richards
G.W. Rose
T. Taylor
J.F. Ward
S. Williams
R. Wilson

NOTE RE-MAPS

Because of the vast extent and shape of the dock systems on both sides of the River Mersey, coupled with the extent and complications of the dockland rail lines, it is not possible to include in a book of this size, maps sufficiently detailed to be of any use. Readers wishing to study the railway track layouts in detail are referred to Ordnance Survey maps held by the museums and libraries of Liverpool, Birkenhead and Wallasey. With the obliteration of most of the railway goods stations and some docks, only consultation of O.S. maps will enable the enquirer of the future to ascertain exactly where these were located, due to redevelopment of the land which they occupied.

Introduction

Although the Mersey docks and shipping have been featured in many books and articles in the press and various journals, very little has been written concerning the extensive internal railway systems on the docks of Liverpool, Bootle, Birkenhead and Wallasey. In view of the complexity of the railways themselves, with their numerous main-line connections, and the vast traffic they handled, the dearth of written material is hard to understand.

It is the hope of the author that this little book will be the precursor of a thorough history of Merseyside's dockland railways and their astonishing variety of locomotives, a subject which, in view of its complexity, must needs be tackled by a team. This one-man task has been a hard one, but a great pleasure - the result of years of dockland wanderings in the days when it was all happening. Hopefully, older readers will find the story nostalgic, whilst the younger readers, observing the scene today, might be tempted to wonder if the dockland was really the busy, teeming, yet romantic place as chronicled here. Indeed, it was!

Liverpool.
May, 1988

CHAPTER ONE

Setting The Scene

Ships, the sea and ocean transport have been associated with Merseyside for such a long period of time that it is quite impossible to visualise the River Mersey's North-Western extremity without the docks that are ranged along it's shores for more than six miles on the East bank, and penetrate deeply inland on the West or Wirral side, on which lay respectively, the ports of Liverpool with Bootle, Birkenhead and Wallasey. Upon surveying the acres of stone, concrete, steel, iron and timber which have been swallowed up in dock construction, one is overwhelmed by the vastness and complexity of the structures which, with herculean toil, have been fashioned from those materials, and with the way of life that came to be associated with them and the ships they harboured. The fact that the docks, quays and adjacent streets occupy land that was once golden sands and fair green countryside can scarcely be imagined, but it took a long time for the transformation to be accomplished indeed, 300 years of history lie in the development of the Mersey ports and their multifarious facilities for trade and commerce.

The very first Liverpool dock - if such it could be could be termed, was formed by enclosing a length of the former Pool to make a sheltered haven for shipping, this task being carried out in the year 1635. The Pool was a creek of the River Mersey which penetrated inland, curving Northwards as it narrowed, terminating in the locality that is today the junction of Dale Street and Byrom Street. Even though ships of the 17th century were small, they could only navigate the creek for a little distance at the riverward end. The broad expanse of Canning Place, which was laid out after the creek had been filled in, occupies the site of the Pool's Western extremity.

The small haven which was made in the creek was eventually developed into a primative dock by the construction of stone quays, and a gate was provided at the river entrance. This work was completed in 1715, under the direction of Thomas Steers, the first of several engineers who built up the docks system over the years. As other docks were constructed and brought into use, the original one, which hitherto was nameless, became known as the Old Dock. It was, of course, limited in capacity, and ever-increasing trade coupled with the growth in the size of ships, made provision of further docks essential. Incidentally, Thomas Steers is commemorated today by

Steers House, the modern complex of buildings that stand upon the site of the first dock, though for a century or so the area was occupied by the famous Liverpool Custom House, an imposingly grand porticoed and domed building that was destroyed during the air raids of 1940-41, a notable landmark that is still missed by older citizens, and which will be referred to again later.

The second dock to be constructed was Salthouse, which became one of the best known of the early docks as it figured in old sea shanties and poetry. Salthouse Dock was opened in 1753, followed by Georges Dock in 1771, the latter built by Henry Berry who was successor to Thomas Steers as Docks Engineer. The Old Dock fell into disuse gradually and eventually became filled with rubbish. It had outlived its usefullness and was completely filled in during 1826. The site was used for the aforementioned Custom House, the foundation stone of which was laid in August, 1828. A similar fate befell Georges Dock, which was drained on 31st July, 1900 and filled in, the area thus reclaimed being used as the site for the Dock Office, Royal Liver and Cunard Buildings.

Other docks built before the railway age were King's and Queen's, in 1788 and 1796 respectively. During the early years of the Nineteenth Century steam marine engines began to be developed, and in 1822 a steam ferry began a service on the Mersey between Queen's Dock and Tranmere. This was a tiny twin-hull paddle steamer named Etna, and the location from which it sailed is still known as the South Ferry Basin. In the ensuing years steam ships became more and more common on the River Mersey, increasing in size as time passed, but it was not until well into the present century that the masts, spars and rigging of the sailing ships of old finally disappeared from the river that once knew them so well, and now, in their turn, steam ships are becoming fewer as the years roll on their relentless course, the heavy oil engine being today's marine power plant.

In 1826 the Salthouse dry dock was rebuilt and upon its re-opening as a "wet" dock received the title of Canning. By this time men of commerce were active in Liverpool and its neighbour, Manchester, promoting a new form of land transport that was to have an enormous effect on trade and travel — namely the railway. The Liverpool and Manchester Railway opened on 15th September, 1830, included an extension in a tunnel beneath the town, from Edge Hill to the dock road at Wapping, and it was inevitable that the rails would be pushed into the dock estate. However, the Docks Committee of the Liverpool Council were cautious about the use of rail transport and some members were absolutely hostile to railways on the dock road and quays, so arguments raged for some time before common sense prevailed and rail transport became accepted by the Dock Trustees, albeit with some reluctance at first.

The first mention of a railway into the dock estate was in April 1831 when the Liverpool and Manchester company applied to the Docks Committee for sanction to extend their line from Wapping goods station into King's Dock, at their own expense. On 8th May of that year Messrs John Cropper, Theodore Rathbone and Henry Booth of the L & M met with the Docks Committee to present plans of the railway etc. The matter took a long time to resolve however as it was not until June, 1835 that permission was granted, and only so long as the line proved advantageous and would be open to use by anyone. Should the railway prove to be a nuisance however, they would order the L & M company to remove the rails and restore the street paving. The line was duly laid, and remained, not having proved the nuisance that the Docks Committee feared.

The Dock Surveyor reported in March 1842 that owing to bad weather conditions, excavations at the site of the future Albert Dock and Canning Dock had been delayed due to the river flats being unable to transport spoil away as quickly as required, and suggested that a rail line extending from Salthouse Dock to the north of Beacons Gutter would be of great assistance in removing spoil. The Docks Committee agreed to this and in due course accepted a tender for the supply of iron rails from John Baker of Chillington Iron Works.

On 11th April, 1844 the Liverpool & Manchester Railway Company received permission from the Dock Trustees to lay rails on the East quay of King's Dock. In the same year the Dock Trustees applied to the Commissioner of Highways for permission to make rail crossings over public streets in the dock area, they themselves having received Parliamentary Powers to lay rails on the docks and quays rather than let private railway companies do so. Some industrial concerns were however, allowed to lay branches or sidings for their own use and usually at their own expense.

During 1845 Jesse Hartley, the docks Chief Engineer, submitted a lengthy memo to the Dock Committee upon the desirability of a railway to traverse the full length of the dock road, with branches serving wharves and quays etc. The committee still seemed a little wary of making railways in the dock area and wrote to dock authorities in other ports including Dublin, enquiring whether or not they had railways serving them. Most of the replies were in the affirmative.

It was of course, obvious that the docks with their ever increasing traffic should be rail served, so construction of the docks railway began in earnest, and by 1851 the line extended from Wapping L&NWR goods depot to Toxteth Dock. In 1852 the line was extended into Brunswick Dock for the mahogany trade.

In March, 1852 Messrs. Duncan Ewing &Co. received permission to lay track through their yard at Brunswick Dock on the condition that the rail line become the property of the Dock Estate at valuation upon the expiration of the lease. In April of the same year, Messrs. Chaloner & Fleming were granted leave to have a line laid into their yard at Brunswick Dock on the same terms that applied to Duncan Ewings. Another extension in 1852 was provision of a line into Huskisson Dock, at the north end to serve timber yards beginning to spread over the area, and a new dock, Canada, was later built mainly for the timber trade.

The year 1853 saw the construction of a line along Wapping from the north end of Queen's Dock to the south end of Canning Dock, but was used only for transporting materials for dock works for a time. Construction of what became the docks 'main line' continued, and by 1860 the railway stretched from Harrington Dock in the south to the then new Canada Dock in the north.

In 1857 a siding was laid at the Harrington Estate for joint use by the London & North Western and Lancashire & Yorkshire Railway companies, each paying half the cost of its construction. Although most of the aforementioned lines were laid by the dock trustees, they did not operate them, it being left to the railway companies and local firms to do so with their own motive power, not locomotives, but horses!

A service unique to Liverpool was the running of horse-drawn omnibuses on the dock rails. These vehicles with retractable flanges on their wheels were the invention of William Curtiss, a London coaching proprietor, he, and others running services between 1852 and 1893, ceasing when the electric overhead railway was opened. The vehicles ran to strict timetables and had to draw off the rails when catching up with a train. They carried something like two million passengers per year.

The foregoing gives, somewhat briefly, the origins of what became an extensive and busy railway system with an ultimate total of 81 miles of track serving the docks of Liverpool and Bootle for 130 years or so, although the final 20 years saw a steady decline to almost extinction.

Not only was the railway used for general merchandise traffic, but in its early years considerable use of it was made in connection with dock construction for transporting materials etc. This traffic became so heavy that it interfered with normal commercial traffic and there were plenty of complaints from merchants whose goods were delayed. Rail traffic on the docks was slow because horse teams were employed for haulage, and continued to be so until 1895, of which more later. This meant that a train only consisted of up to eight small-capacity wagons. Locomotives were employed by the main-line railway companies within the confines of their dockside goods stations, and very occasionally an engine was allowed on the dock road for special traffic, usually for short periods only under strict conditions.

Busy as the dock railway became, its development was rather slow except for the 'main line'. Extensions were carried out bit by bit, a siding here, a branch there, usually after much discussion by the Railway and Traffic Committees. It took a war to get extra line capacity provided, starting in World War One during which the Ministry of Shipping ordered extra sidings to be laid at Queen's Dock, Hornby Dock and elsewhere on the estate. After that war and in the years up to World War Two, quite a lot of new lines were laid on dock quays and to serve the extended Gladstone Dock system completed in 1927.

In World War Two the rail system was strained to the limit, whilst also having to contend with heavy air raids which inflicted great damage on the docks. Extra sidings were laid alongside the timber yard at Sandhills Lane, and on Muspratts Estate at Seaforth Sands. Extra lines were provided also at Toxteth Dock on its east side. Consideration was given to providing an extra line along the dock road, but to make room for such, the Liverpool Overhead Railway would need to have been removed and that system was vitally needed to carry dock workers and ships crews speedily up and down the docks, so no extra line was made. The Overhead Railway was repeatedly damaged during the air raid period from August 1940 to May 1941 and this caused some interuption to traffic on the docks railway running directly below the overhead structure.

The track structure of the early dockside railways in Liverpool consisted of lightweight iron rails laid on longitudinal timbers, with the granite setts or cobblestones, the latter known as boulder paving, laid flush with the rail-head. At first trouble was experienced through wheel flanges striking the paving, so some means had to be found to prevent this happening. As the grooved girder rail familiar in street tramway practice had not been devised, it was necessary to employ a second but narrower rail on the inside so as to provide a clear flangeway. Some lengths of this early track including points and crossings with an abundance of ironwork survived into the 1980's at Canning Dock, whilst at Nelson Dock a scissors crossing of sharp radius survived into the 1960's. Both examples have long been disused as they would not take modern locomotives or rolling stock. In 1859 iron rails were supplied to the Mersey Docks & Harbour Board by Bailey Bros. and the Ebbw Vale Company, the above-named surviving examples probably being part of that contract.

These ancient iron rails, black with disuse, form a link with early railway days and lie quietly awaiting their fate, unheeded by all except railway historians and industrial archaeologists seeking to provide records of industry's yesteryears. The rails used in more recent years were of special heavy-section 126.2 lb grooved girder type, which are simply a much heavier version of the familiar street tramway rails but designed specially for Liverpool and Birkenhead docks to withstand the wear and tear of heavy traffic. Along the "main line" which traversed the full length of the dock roadway, extensive use was made of welding in recent times, eliminating hundreds of rail joints with their potential to work loose. Welding provided a continuous, smooth surface. Girder rails began to be used for track renewals in 1908.

Although steam locomotives were used almost universally by the main-line railway companies and hauled trains to and from the numerous goods stations that were ranged along the Liverpool dock estate, the port authorities would not permit steam locomotives to work along the dockside lines. In earlier times fires of spectacular enormity and with extremely destructive results were quite common among dock sheds, warehouses and timber yards, and it was the constant fear that sparks thrown from the chimneys of hardworking locomotives would contribute to the fire hazard that caused the authorities to insist on the employment of horses for hauling railway wagons in the docks area — a state of affairs that lasted as late as 1895. It was mainly due to the ever-increasing traffic volume that eventually exceeded the capacity of "horse-power" and threatened chaos which caused the rule to be waived and locomotives with suitable spark-arresting devices allowed to enter the docks, although the first to do so were oil-burners.

Regrettably, Liverpool's once extensive and busy dock railway system must, with the exception of a small portion, be referred to in the past tense because, although its rails still largely exist within the dock estate, the system is devoid of life and the only stretches in use at the present are between Alexandra Dock and the Seaforth container base, and a short line into Hornby Dock. Of course, the port has suffered a severe decline in common with most of the other old-established sea-ports of Britain and road vehicles take most of the traffic to and from the few docks that remain in use.

Railways serving seaports all have their particular characteristecs. For instance, the London system was mainly inside the dock walls, whilst on Clydeside the rails threaded the public streets in certain places, and until recent times the locomotives shared the rails with the Glasgow city electric trams. Neither London or Liverpool could provide the fascinating Glasgow spectacle of a tram followed by a goods train loaded with steel for ship-building, but in Liverpool the docks "main line" followed the dock road, sometimes within and sometimes outside the dock walls, and crossed some of the city's busiest streets on the level in the vicinity of the Pier Head. In that locality too, its rails intersected those of the Liverpool tramways in three places, and the shadow of its companion, the Overhead Railway, obscured the sunshine from those same rails for a period of no less than 63 years. Branches penetrated along the quays and wharves of most of the docks, whilst others struck off across the busy dock road, vanishing into industrial buildings, the cavernous gloom of railway goods stations, or passed along granite-setted streets between the towering, vast brickwork of warehouses. At Queens, Trafalgar, Huskisson, Alexandra and Gladstone Docks rails ran along the river wall in exposed locations at which a train could be drenched with spray when the Mersey was in one of its turbulent moods, but for the most part the rails ran along the quays beside the calm waters of the sheltered docks.

The rails which traversed the vast area of Liverpool and Birkenhead docks were laid in a considerable variety of surfaces. The oldest, of which a few lengths can still be found, are embedded in large cobblestones. Others are laid in granite setts, and on these sections the horses that hauled the wagons in pre-locomotive days were able to dig their hooves into the spaces between in order to get a good grip. Newer and recently re-laid sections of track reposed in smooth, flush concrete. Trackwork of endless variety was encountered at junctions, which were numerous, and sharp curves which could be negotiated only by locomotives with a short wheelbase, abounded. The streets of the dock area are mostly quite narrow, and contain industrial premises of great variety — transport and goods depots, stores, warehouses, pubs on the corners and a surprising number of dwelling houses and shops varying in vintage from a century old to recent. The wartime air raids on the port destroyed hundreds of buildings and left many gaps in the scene, but rebuilding has filled most of them up again. In the 1970's and 1980's greater gaps were being created by ball-swinging cranes and bulldozers as the great, deserted warehouses were demolished, some of them being tough, hard work to remove due to the strength and quality of the materials and the workmanship put into them in the far-distant days when they were built. Changed transport methods and means of distribution have brought about their demise.

Until recent times the docks were populated daily by thousands of men, and many women too, engaged on the vast variety of tasks called for in a busy seaport. On the riverward side of the main dock road ships dominated the scene along with towering cranes and dockside transit sheds. On a normal weekday when business was in full swing, the docks were a hive of intense activity. Today's traffic is almost entirely in motor vehicles, but for a long period of time steam wagons, horse-drawn drays and trains formed a major part of the scene. Steam, and latterly diesel locomotives slogged away among the road traffic with their heavy loads. Whistles shrieked and bells tolled, wheel flanges whined and screeched, wagons rattled and shuddered along, a clanking of buffers heralding a halt to await a clear passage across an intersection. Steam was the motive power for 60 years and the neat but tough locomotives puffed lustily along, their warning bells tolling continuously as they travelled whilst the later diesel machines, introduced after World War Two, burbled and chanted, their coupling rods churning slowly. These engines likewise were equipped with warning bells. For so many years the rails were polished by the endless passage of wheels, but some sections lay dull with disuse, the industry or dock which they served having been abandoned due to the ever changing pattern of commercial activity, or through war damage. Sometimes a length of track would be out of use for years, the rail grooves becoming packed solid with dust and rubbish in which weeds and grass flourished, only to be suddenly traversed by a train once more as a new turn in the fortunes of the locality once again warranted rail traffic.

In many places along the docks one may come across a track crossing the main road and ending abruptly at a fence or brick wall or disappearing into a mound of weed-covered earth and rubble. These relics of another era recall the wartime blitz — those grim nights of 1940 and 1941 when the port was under aerial attack and took a severe hammering. Many warehouses and railway goods stations were entirely destroyed or extensively damaged during the blitz and so many dockside installations wrecked that the work of the port was severely handicapped. Roads and railway tracks lay buried in rubble, and large numbers of railway wagons and road vehicles were destroyed. Ships were sunk, cranes twisted and sheds blasted, fires raged for days on end and frenzied efforts were made to restore order and keep things moving. Nevertheless, despite overwhelming odds, the port never came to a standstill and it was amazing to see how quickly determination and improvisation achieved results. It was a heartening sight after a night of terror, and while fires were still burning, to see amid the rubble and debris a Saddle Tank locomotive making its way along with a train in tow, the crew often having to climb down to heave some obstruction from the rails. However, some of the destroyed railway depots were never rebuilt and the land they stood on has been subsequently used for other purposes.

The fascination of the docks was boundless, as quite apart from ships and trains there existed a multitude of other things and activities ranging from the realm of industrial archaeology to the ultra-modern and scientific. To take the former, we have the romantic atmosphere that is all pervading in the locale of the oldest docks such as Canning, Albert and Salthouse to which (until closure) the old time aura still clung, despite manifestations of modernism and the huge city that has grown behind them. These old docks have for years been used only by small vessels, their old sandstone and granite quays and ancient sheds and warehouses preserving in some measure the atmosphere of the days of sailing ships — a great contrast to the Northernmost docks with their vast size, modern equipment and capacity for accommodating the largest ships afloat. Once a person had been captivated by the romance of the river frontage the interest was never lost. Talk of ships was incessant in the dockside pubs, canteens and those little cafes that are quaintly called cocoa rooms, and has been so since mercantile business began. Such shop talk is likely to continue until the last vessel sails away from this city of shipping.

Cargoes dealt with at great ports such as Liverpool and Birkenhead embraced almost everything used by mankind, from timber to machinery, from locomotives to oil drums — items large and small. Foodstuffs too, came through the docks, and commodities such as cotton, tobacco and oil. The list is endless. Vast transit sheds through which cargo passed constantly were a feature of most of the docks, whilst more recently container bases have reduced the need for warehouses, though some of these still remain. In some locations, container depots occupy ground on which warehouses once reared their mighty bulk, but had outlived their usefulness.

Merseyside is the second largest grain milling centre of the world, the twin cities of St. Paul and Minneapolis in the U.S.A. taking first place. Most of the mills are on the Birkenhead and Wallasey dock estate and once used rail transport extensively. Flocks of pigeons flutter around the enormous flour-streaked and often gloomy looking corn mills and warehouses, whilst seagulls wheel and screech overhead, to contribute to the multifarious sounds of the port along with the shouts of the dock workers, the ships' sirens and the rattle of cranes. The solid roar of motor vehicles has replaced the hissing of steam wagons and the clip-clop of hooves that were sounds that gradually faded and ceased finally after the close of World War 2.

The sweet aromas and pungent smells contributed to the fascination of dockland districts in every port — the salty tang of sea air, the smell of tar, hemp, oil, creosote, coal smoke, steam, petrol and diesel fumes. All these are of ships and transport. A whiff of the Orient came from spices and pepper, whilst nuts and molasses called other far places to mind. Tobacco has a popular scent but some of the industrial smells were not so pleasant and one was glad to get past such places as seed mills, tanning works and so on! Such was the variety of industry and commerce to be found in the fascinating world of the waterfront!

The visitor to the docks saw so many different things that trying to recall them resulted in only a jumble in the mind. Even a hundred visits would not suffice to mentally digest it all. Most vivid among the impressions gained would be ships and people. One looked with fascination at the docks, harbouring ships of many kinds and sizes, belonging to many nations, each owning company having its particular colours and house flag. The calls and banter of the dock workers were heard, there were slogans to read chalked on walls, religious messages and otherwise, notices to mariners giving details of forthcoming ship launches or hazards to navigation and the names of shipping lines on dock sheds to claim attention. The passing traffic was continuous in movement and visitors had always to be on the alert for their own safety amid all this activity.

The progressive modernisation of the docks has, year by year, eliminated so much that was old and obsolete, but it was a gradual process. Some objects from the past survived long after their purpose was no longer called for, among them being the water columns at intervals along the dock road, which quenched the thirsts of hardworking horses and filled the tanks of the numerous steam wagons. Lots of these survived until fairly recently. Then there are the old guns stuck muzzle-downward into the ground to serve as posts for safety chains — what long ago ships and wars did these serve in? Most incongruous of the dockside buildings however, are those tall, battlemented towers built in grey granite that add a fairy-tale touch to the scene in the older docks. These, built by the versatile docks engineer Jesse Hartley, date from the 1840's and once contained hydraulic machinery for working swing bridges and dock gates. The long dockside sheds with their granite walls in cyclopean or crazy-paving pattern are further curiosities from the days of long ago, and so also are the conical stone towers that served as police or time-keeper's shelters. Tall brick chimneys, many of quite ornate design still tower above defunct hydraulic power houses in various places along the docks, relics of a once extensive power system now replaced by electrical machinery.

The foregoing, though not directly relevant to railways, is intended to set the scene into which the now vanished dockside lines fitted in their own distinctive way; they cannot be considered in isolation even though they possessed a character and fascination probably unequalled in any other port. To explore the complete system was a task of considerable magnitude and could occupy many days. The following chapter deals with the extensive railway system that served the docks for their full length, from Seaforth Sands in the north to Herculaneum Dock at the south end of the city.

Avonside 0-6-0 Saddle Tank No. 26 at Huskisson Dock. May 1960.
Photo — T. Taylor

Avonside 0-6-0 Saddle Tank No. 16 at Princes Dock in May, 1959. In th: background is ex-LNWR 0-8-0 No. 49173 returning to Edge Hill after working a train to Riverside Station.   Photo — J.A. Peden

Steam wagons were once a familiar sight on Liverpool's dock road. Here is one of the last remaining vehicles passing Tower Building in 1959.
Photo — J.A. Peden

All trains stop here! The end of the line at Queen's Dock in 1960. An extension beyond this point was planned but did not materialise. River Mersey and skyline of Birkenhead in the background. Photo — T. Taylor

Liverpool Tram No. 185 about to cross the docks railway at the foot of James Street. A busy location at which almost every form of transport could be seen including the famous Overhead Railway. Photographed in August 1955.
Photo — R.B. Parr

A busy quayside scene with an Avonside 0-6-0 Saddle Tank engine slogging along. Photo — J.A. Peden

Herculaneum Dock 1956. Liverpool Overhead Railway train crossing the bridge that leads to Dingle Tunnel. Photo — J.A. Peden

14

CHAPTER TWO

Before The Liners Left Us

We now venture on a walking tour of the Liverpool and Bootle docks, but we must necessarily turn the calendar back to the period following the end of World War 2 when so much of the pre-war scene remained, except for gaps caused by the air-raids, and when the docks and railways were complete and busy. Since that time vast changes have taken place in Merseyside's docklands, extensive rebuilding, modernisation and more recently, closures having swept away so much that was once familiar, and in this process the greater part of the dockside railway and its environment have vanished. In view of these changes, a description of the docks as they are today would give no hint of the one-time enormous importance of the railways in the business of the port, which continued for some years after the end of the war. Here then is the scene as it was in the years 1946 — 1948 etc.

The most convenient place to begin a dockland exploration is Seaforth Sands, at which the dock system reaches its most northerly extent. This is a busy place so far as transportation is concerned, as it is a terminus for several Liverpool Corporation tram and bus services, also a staging point for buses of the Ribble Company which connect Liverpool with such places as Waterloo, Crosby and beyond. Moreover, "Sands" is an important station on the Liverpool Overhead Railway, whose plate-girder bridge spans Crosby Road South alongside a similar bridge that carries the Aintree — North Mersey Branch goods railway line. There is a busy junction formed by the intersection of Regent Road, Knowsley Road, Crosby Road South and Rimrose Road. Needless to say motor traffic is very heavy at this point. In order to reach the docks it is necessary to turn into Fort Road which runs from Crosby Road to the river frontage, and passes between two buildings belonging to the Overhead Railway — the Seaforth Sands station on the left-hand side, and the carriage sheds and workshops of that system on the right-hand side. The most notable features that strike the eye here are the enormous concrete transit sheds of Gladstone Dock, topped by rows of powerful cranes that tower upwards high above the ships moored alongside the quays. The extensive Gladstone system of docks was completed in two stages, in 1913 and 1927 and they can accommodate the largest ships afloat. Before these docks were constucted the area was occupied by brickfields, these being served by branches from the docks railway.

The fresh breeze and tang of sea air make themselves felt at the corner of the dock road, this section of the long highway being named Shore Road. Here a sudden and surprising vista springs into view — the yellow sands stretching away northwards, the wide Mersey estuary, also the resort of New Brighton directly opposite. Beyond, in the distance, the hills of North Wales form the backcloth to a pleasant scene. Close at hand however, are the wide gateways to the dock estate and here we pause for a moment to admire the ocean passenger ships moored alongside the quays, or standing high and dry in the deep graving dock, being repaired and repainted ready for further voyages. At this time many are finishing their wartime service as troop transports, their all-over drab grey paint now being replaced by new peacetime colours and their luxurious furnishings restored ready for them to convey civilian passengers once again. Nobody gives any thought to the possibility that the era of the ocean liner might be drawing to a gradual close — all seems bright in the passenger shipping world at this time!

To the north of Gladstone Dock there stretches an extensive "field" in which there are over fifty railway sidings laid with flat-bottom type rails, and upon these lines stand large numbers of open goods wagons used for internal purposes within the dock estate. Many of them are in good, serviceable condition, in the red livery of the MD & HB, whilst others are in advanced stages of dilapidation. A large proportion of these wagons are ancient specimens with dumb buffers (timber blocks and no springs) and thus barred from entering upon a main line. This land is partly graveyard, partly limbo and also a repair centre. Other items of dock equipment — old steam cranes, locomotives, boilers, road vehicles including horse drays and so on repose among the grass and weeds. From time to time repaired wagons and machinery emerge from this limbo gleaming in new paint. To the north of the field large stacks of cut timber are stored, with railway tracks passing between them, all terminating at buffer-stops behind the high wooden fence that borders Crosby Road South. This large expanse of land was formerly part of Muspratt's estate which surrounded Seaforth Hall, a large "country house", built in 1840, which was the home of James Muspratt, the chemicals magnate in days long gone. It was demolished in 1924.

Proceeding onwards, the next item of interest is an ugly iron bridge with solid plated sides, which carries the LMS (formerly L & Y) North Mersey Branch line over the Dock Road, immediately adjacent to its junction with Regent Road, the last named becoming the dock road itself from here onwards. The North Mersey Branch, curving sharply is now on the right, descending gradually to street level on a series of stonework arches which reduce in height progressively as the railway comes lower, and upon reaching road level the tracks fan out into the numerous sidings of the North Mersey goods yard. To the left lie extensive timber yards with their high stacks of cut timbers, and the whine of circular saws at work assails our ears as we traverse this corner of dockland. The motor traffic is not heavy on this section of Regent Road, which is separated from the docks by the above-mentioned railway yard. Vehicles for Gladstone Dock enter the dock estate at Seaforth Sands or at the foot of Strand Road, further along, leaving only through traffic or that for the timber yards to use this stretch of road. The most notable object in the immediate vicinity is the Goliath cantilever crane in North Mersey yard, which was installed in 1908. Its lifting capacity is 10 tons, the span being of 172 feet. However, the crane is little used nowadays and it is destined to be cut up for scrap (this took place in 1952).

The North Mersey yard and goods depot were opened in 1866 and enabled the Lancashire & Yorkshire Railway company to get a foothold in the North Docks — actually they anticipated further dock expansion because at that time the newest docks were the Canada group, about a mile distant, the first of these docks being opened in 1859. Thus the yard was bordered by sand dunes and fields when first built, but it was not long before the tide of stone, bricks and iron spread over the district, and it is difficult to imagine sandhills in today's industrial environment.

On the riverward side of North Mersey yard is Hornby Dock which was opened in 1884 and which was the last of the great docks built until ever-larger passenger liners forced construction of what became the Gladstone group completed in 1927. Hornby locomotive shed of the MD & HB; built to accommodate ten locomotives is situated at the North end of the dock. It was erected in 1918, to house and service extra locomotives purchased during World War 1 to handle the large volume of traffic engendered by that lengthy conflict.

Reverting back to North Mersey yard, generally two or three steam locomotives are likely to be present at most times of the day or evening, various types appearing in addition to the usual 0-6-0 Saddle Tank engines of Lancashire & Yorkshire Railway origin. "Trip engines" work between Aintree and North Mersey day and night. The vast marshalling yards at Aintree were developed in the 1880's to serve the docks, an enormous coal traffic for export and bunkering being handled as well as general merchandise. Day and night lengthy coal trains trundled towards Aintree from mines in Lancashire and Yorkshire hauled by massive eight-coupled locomotives.

A few moments steady walking brings us to the gates of the Langton Dock goods yard of the former Midland Railway, which is linked to North Mersey yard by a single line that crosses Regent Road at an acute angle. Langton yard is at the end of a branch line from Fazakerly North Junction on the CLC Aintree-Halewood North Junction line. This branch was opened in 1885. The yard is actually some distance from the dock after which it is named, its title being thus something of a misnomer. Rails, but not of Midland origin do of course, continue onwards to Langton Dock, which was opened by H.R.H. the Prince of Wales on 8th September, 1881, but the dock adjacent to Langton railway depot is actually Hornby Dock. In order to reach Langton from the North, the Midland company made use of their Running Powers over the Lancashire & Yorkshire Railway between Hellifield and Aintree, thence over the Cheshire Lines system to Walton-on-the-Hill, the final stretch being their own line from the latter place to Langton Dock depot. Additionally, the Midland reached their other depot at Sandon Dock via the Halewood North Junction — Walton — Huskisson line of the Cheshire Lines railway in which the Midland was a partner along with the Great Northern and Great Central Railways.

Both the North Mersey and Langton yards are linked to the lines of the Mersey Docks & Harbour Board by rails crossing Regent Road. North Mersey yard is entirely open to the elements, no covered accommodation being provided, but there is a fair-sized administration building and goods office at its South-East corner near Strand Road. Langton M R Yard has an office building and goods shed almost opposite the L & Y block. This yard is backed by Rimrose Road, at higher level, which crosses its approach lines on a series of stone arches. All streets running East — West slope quite steeply down to the river front in this area. The Great Western Railway Company maintain a goods depot at Langton — the most Northerly of G.W.R. goods stations, served only by road motors as there is no rail access. Nearby streets containing enormous warehouses are named after oceans — Atlantic Road, Pacific Road, Arctic Road etc.

Langton yard ends at Lyster Road (named after George F. Lyster, Chief Dock Engineer 1861-1897) but three parallel lines emerge from a gateway and cross this road continuing through stone-setted Arctic Road between the tall, old, fortress-like buildings of the Alexandra Granary, a grim but fascinating place which is operated by the Liverpool Grain Storage & Transit Company. Rails laid in the street run beneath the colonades of the granary, large iron turntables laid flush with the road surface enabling access to large doorways in the buildings through which the rails penetrate into dark, mysterious-looking passages. Grain dust streaks the buildings and hordes of pigeons perpetually frequent the place and keep themselves well fed on the spillage from vehicles. Railway wagons and motor lorries load-up at this establishment, the grain being transmitted into the vehicles through flexible pipes from overhead hoppers. At this time the granary is busy, but it is destined to cease operations a few years hence. Another notable building on the riverward side of the dock road is the Union Cold Storage depot which provides a great deal of meat traffic for the railways, a fact apparent from the lines of refrigerator vans on the dockside tracks.

The rails that pass through Arctic Road emerge to cross Strand Road and enter the Alexandra Dock goods yard of the former London & North Western Railway. This yard is in three sections, the northerly and smallest section being separated from the extensive main yard by Church Street, over which a double track passes and rather unusually for this area, the crossing is protected by regular level crossing gates worked from a small signal box, a standard L & NWR timber-built structure situated north of the crossing on the Regent Road side of the line. For many years the north yard has dealt mainly with grain traffic which is worked away from the yard via the Edge Hill — Bootle Branch.

The main Alexandra Dock goods depot is extensive. Before the 1939 war a large brick-and-iron-built warehouse occupied the dock road side of the yard, but was destroyed by bombing. This multi-storey building was replaced by a new single-storey shed after the war. Connection with the dockside railway is made by a double track crossing Regent Road at the north end, and further along by a heavily used double-track also crossing Regent Road and curving in a northerly direction. A little-way south of this a single track comes directly out of the yard and leads straight across the main road into the docks, crossing the main docks line by right-angle crossings. The third and most southerly section of Alexandra yard had very sharp curves and is worked only by 0-4-0 Tank locomotives. This too, has a double track connection with the docks railway, crossing Regent Road and curving southwards as it does so. All these crossings are laid in stone setts with bull-head rails accompanied by heavy check rails.

On the west side of the dock road two big grain silos are prominent features of Alexandra Dock. These are owned by the Liverpool Grain Storage & Transit Co. Floating grain elevators in the docks suck the grain from the ships holds and deliver it into the silos.

Reverting to the corner of Strand Road for a moment, it is here that the dock road, having passed between railway and timber yards from Seaforth Sands now comes right alongside the docks. The road is fairly straight but here the docks of the Alexandra group penetrate further inland than the Gladstone and Hornby docks and thus come close to Regent Road, as also do all the other docks south of this point right through to the southern extremity at Dingle. At the foot of Lyster Road two single lines leading in different directions make a diamond crossing right in the centre of Regent Road, so that trains coming onto the dock estate from Langton yard travel along the main highway for some little distance, among the motor traffic.

Alexandra Dock is the terminus for a passenger train service to and from Liverpool, Lime Street, introduced in 1881 but now infrequent. The station with its glass canopy on iron columns is seen on the left. The Liverpool Overhead Railway which follows the dock road for almost its entire length, is on the right-hand side of the road as we proceed southwards, and has a station at Alexandra Dock. Every few moments an "Overhead" train rumbles past carrying the dock workers, seafarers, and the sightseers, the latter whom come in their hundreds to observe the panorama of dockland. This is a district of sheds, high warehouses, industrial buildings, stores, shops, pubs, cafes of varying quality and garages, and this kind of "scenery" will be with us for the full length of our walk. Numerous side streets lead down to the dock road, all much the same in character though the ages of the buildings differ, and so do the architectural styles, from ancient to modern.

The southern section of Alexandra railway yard is actually situated opposite to Langton Dock, which has already been mentioned in connection with the Midland Railway branch line, but the L & NW company called their station Atlantic Dock initially, as this was the name by which Alexandra Dock was to be known before the decision to name it after H.R.H. Princess Alexandra, who opened it on 8th September 1881 (the same day on which Langton Dock was opened). The original title is still used by the LMS Railway Company at Atlantic Dock Junction, Bootle, at which the Edge Hill — North Docks line divides to serve Alexandra and Canada Docks. This line is known as the Bootle Branch.

A large and magnificent hydraulic pumping station is a prominent feature of Langton Dock. Designed by G. F. Lyster, it was completed in 1879 ready for the opening of the new dock.

The next important thoroughfare that joins Regent Road is Miller's Bridge, which takes its title from a bridge over the Leeds & Liverpool Canal nearby. At the foot of this street lie the busy docks of the Brocklebank group, the Brocklebank station of the Overhead Railway being almost opposite the road junction. The first of this group of docks was opened in 1881.

Miller's Bridge was named after a solicitor, William Spurstow Miller who had a fine mansion built adjacent to what was then a sandy beach in the late 17th century. The house resembled a castle with battlemented towers and acquired the nickname of "Bootle Castle" but was usually known as "Millers Castle". It was still in situ when the dock road and railway were extended northwards in the 1850's and the shore being developed into docks and quays, on land claimed from the Mersey. The "Castle" stood on the south side of Miller's bridge. Today Effingham Street occupies its former site.

A shed for accommodating 12 locomotives is situated at Brocklebank Dock, being the largest depot on the MD & HB railway system. It was opened in 1916. After 30 years of use, it was replaced by a new shed in 1946.

The next item of railway interest is reached after passing Howe Street. Here, the works of Messrs. Harland & Wolff, of shipbuilding fame are situated — an ornately fronted building with a wide arch through which passes a single track branch line from the docks railway which curves across Regent Road. Another works belonging to the same organisation is situated a little way southwards and extends for almost a block between Drake and Raleigh Streets. This latter works has no rail connection however. Quickly following on Raleigh Street is Dacre Street and beyond it are the works of Messrs. T. W. Ward Ltd., metal merchants, a single track branch from the docks railway curving across Regent Road and entering through a doorway in the building.

On the riverward side of Regent Road here, is the North Carriers Dock, followed by the several docks of the extensive Canada group of which the first was opened in September 1859 to serve the timber trade. The first ship to enter was the Cunard steamer "Asia", one of those brave, early paddle steamers that had masts and sails in addition to its engines.

There were many timber yards in the vicinity of Canada Dock in the 1860's, and one merchant, R. J. Jones had a line from the dock railway to serve his yard opposite North Carriers Dock which was laid at his expense in 1870. Both yard and rail line have long since vanished.

On the east side of Regent Road there stand a number of industrial buildings which occupy a site originally known as North Dock Yard, and near the south end of the block is the remains of a goods station which was opened by the Great Central Railway on 1st March 1907, followed a month later by a cold storage depot. The depot was bombed during the war and not rebuilt. A single line of grooved rails still curves across Regent Road to enter the former premises, which are bounded on their south side by a street with rural connotations — Lower Bank View, but in reality is occupied by industrial premises and warehouses. No longer is it possible to see a locomotive owned by the London & North Eastern Railway steaming along the dock road between the G.C. yard and the Cheshire Lines depot at Brunswick Dock at the south end of the dock estate. The site of the goods depot is now used as a storage ground by the Mersey Docks & Harbour Board.

Brunswick Place, a street which joins the dock road nearby forms the north boundary of a very extensive railway yard and goods depots — Bankfield and Canada, built by the former Lancashire & Yorkshire Railway Company and reached by a branch from the Liverpool — Southport line at Bootle (Oriel Road) station. The branch was opened in 1887 but before that date the yards, opened in 1868 were accessible from the docks railway. Three branches from the main dockside line laid in grooved rails cross the road to serve these depots, which were heavily damaged in the air-raids of 1940-41 with much loss of rolling stock. The southern end of the railway yard is bounded by Bankfield Street. Construction of the Bankfield & Canada goods stations obliterated Brunswick Street, which ran parallel with the dock road between Brunswick Place and Bankfield Street. A large country house — "Stanley Hall", was demolished to make way for the railway yards. Before Canada Branch Dock No. 1 was developed, a roadway named Battery Street ran from Regent Road towards the river frontage, upon which stood an old fortress, a relic of the days when Liverpool was possibly subject to attack from enemy warships sailing through the Mersey estuary. Near the river there stood for many years a huge castellated hydraulic pumping station which was designed by Jesse Hartley in his usual whimsical style. Sadly, it was demolished recently and the dock lost a magnificent piece of industrial architecture.

Almost opposite the foot of Bankfield Street stands the Canada Dock station of the Overhead railway, situated in a very busy area with the ceaseless activity and traffic making cautious walking imperative. The extensive yards, goods station and passenger station of the former London & North Western Railway occupy a considerable length of Regent Road here. These are at the termination of the Edge Hill — Bootle Branch which was completed through to Canada Dock in 1866. Both the L & NW and L & Y yards are crossed by Derby Road, also Bank Hall Lane and Forth Street by a series of brick arch bridges. The Leeds-Liverpool Canal crosses at high level here. The railway lines, which emerge from tunnels are at the level of the dock road but the side streets (east-west) slope steeply upwards from the dock road to the inland north-south arteries. Road vehicles entering the yard at the docks end have a level run-in, but vehicles entering from Derby Road descend a steep incline.

The single-platform passenger station at Canada Dock, with its building up on Derby Road was closed in May 1941, due to extensive air raid damage extending over the whole of the railway premises, which included total destruction of the vast goods warehouse, a bricks and iron structure, debris from which buried rails and hindered operations. The canal bank was also breached and water cascaded down into the railway yard. An LMS engine, an 0-8-4 Tank had to make a hasty exit lest the rising water put its fire out! Speedy clearance soon got the depot working again, but passenger traffic was not resumed.

Two separate single-line connections between the Canada yards and the docks railway curve in opposite directions across Regent Road, and these are frequently traversed by Dock Board locomotives exchanging traffic with the main-line system. When these trains are required to cross the highway, members of the crew armed with red flags hold up road traffic, which screeches to an impatient halt, losing not a second in moving off again as soon as the rail movement is completed!

Canada Dock itself was originally built for the timber trade, but today handles a variety of traffic. It was also for many years a ship-coaling centre, at which large cranes lifted railway wagons on cradles and swung them out above the ships bunkers into which their contents were tipped, a dusty operation now in decline as more and more ships burn oil instead of coal. The north quay of Canada Branch Dock No. 3 is on the boundary between the Borough of Bootle and the City of Liverpool.

In the 1860's when Canada was the last dock, the land beyond on the riverward side, made up for future dock construction was a vast open space with railway lines wandering over it and narrow channels from the river here and there. The only building on this land was a mortar mill, but timber was stacked here also. The timber yards had railway sidings, and there was a small engine shed on the west side of Regent Road, probably for a contractor's locomotive engaged on construction work.

Canada Dock goods station was built over part of the grounds of "Bank Hall", a large country house which had been demolished years beforehand, and at the time of its construction the area was still partially rural as the tide of building had not yet swept every field and tree away. Also covering the grounds are the warehouses of Juniper Street, Miskelly Street, Barr Street, etc., and various industrial premises, and not a tree or plant in sight. The old hall is commemorated by Bank Hall Street and Bank Hall Lane.

Some little distance south of Canada Dock goods station a single-line spur from the dockside railway curves across Regent Road and passes through a gateway beyond which a group of lengthy parallel sidings lead off, extending to Derby Road. Refrigerator vans for meat traffic are the normal occupants of these sidings, being stabled conveniently close to Canada Dock station which has a meat-handling platform known as the Beef Quay. These sidings were originally provided for timber traffic, and some of this traffic is still dealt with here as stacks of imported timber testify. We also note the large red-leaded storage tanks which hold molasses, with the strong aroma of that substance reminding us of the treacle sandwiches we ate when we were children. The molasses tanks occupy an enclosed yard situated at the north corner of Sandhills Lane.

On the riverward side of the road lie the docks of the Huskisson group, the first of which was opened in 1852, followed by enlargement in 1860 and thereafter. in 1852 a fort and barracks were built at the north-west corner of Huskisson Dock but they have long since vanished.

The area we are now traversing was once the shores of Bootle Bay, and the curvature of the dock road generally indicates that a bay existed but docks built on land claimed from the river have straightened the coast somewhat. Here too was a small inlet from the Mersey known as Beacon's Gutter, now filled in. There were rocks in the river in this vicinity — Salton's Rocks on which not a few ships were wrecked in days of old.

At Huskisson Dock was erected the first locomotive shed for the MD & HB Traffic Department, in 1907. Accommodating six engines, it was built by Messrs E. F. Blakely & Co., and was of corrugated iron construction. The shed is still in use.

Leaving behind us the molasses tanks, the intersection of Sandhills Lane and Regent Road is reached, and beyond this point a complex system of railway lines exists. Huskisson Overhead Railway station is on the right, whilst to the left extends the large Sandon Dock goods station with its vast warehouse in rich red-coloured brickwork. This was built by the former Midland Railway Company, and the extensive yard with its many tracks and turntables has a single-line connection with the docks railway which crosses over Regent Road at an acute angle. The east side of Sandon yard is parallelled by Derby Road (formerly named Victoria Road), over which a single track passes, crossing a double track line of the Liverpool Corporation Tramways and joining the rails of the Cheshire Lines Committee's system in Victoria Yard, which is opposite the Sandon yard. A connection runs thence through a tunnel beneath the main LMS lines out of Liverpool Exchange station (which pass above on a wide embankment on which is situated Sandhills station) and joins the extensive tracks of the CLC Huskisson goods station, on the east side of which is the Leeds & Liverpool Canal, whilst behind this waterway is busy Commercial Road with its mixed industrial and residential character. Although Sandon yard was a Midland Railway establishment, it was 30 miles or so from its parent system, being reached via the Cheshire Lines Railway.

Sandon Dock, named after Lord Sandon, was opened in 1851, and is on our right as we proceed along Regent Road which here curves from its south-westerly course to run due south for some distance. Adjoining Sandon Midland yard, on the south side of Boundary Street, is the extensive North Docks goods station built by the Lancashire & Yorkshire Railway in 1848, which is connected with the Midland establishment by rails crossing the streets. North Docks goods station is at street level and is approached from the high-level main lines on viaducts by a steep incline. A branch runs into the docks here serving coal tips. Originally known as the High Level Coal Railway, it reaches Bramley-Moore and Wellington Docks, and was opened as follows: North Docks Station to Wellington Dock on 23rd December 1856, an extension alongside Bramley-Moore being opened in 1882. Horse haulage of wagons was practised until 1895.

On 19th September 1850, a deputation of colliery proprietors led by William Laird approached the dock authority for increased accommodation for the expanding coal traffic. At a meeting of the Dock Railway Committee held on 2nd March 1852 it was "resolved that a high-level railway to join the curve connecting it with the Lancashire & Yorkshire Railway near the boundary gate of the Sandon Dock and stopping short at the south quay of the Bramley-Moore Dock can be constructed at an estimated cost of £30,550".

In 1851 Liverpool coal exports and consumption by river steamers totalled 405,000 tons, and it was increasing at a fast rate, hence the demand for the new line and coal tipping apparatus.

In 1853 it was realised that the engineer John Grantham's plan for a high-level passenger line along the docks had to be taken into account, so Jesse and John B. Hartley were requested to report on whether such a line would interfere with the High-Level Coal Railway. They considered that it would not do so. Grantham's line was not built, however. Time was passing and traffic increasing, and as the Dock Authority had not made any move towards construction of the coal railway, the L & Y Company applied for leave to build it, and suggested that the line should pass over Regent Road by a lifting bridge which could be raised to permit high loads to pass beneath, and approach the dock estate near the boundary gates of Bramley-Moore and Wellington Docks. This was approved by the dock authority.

In May 1855 a tender from G. Armstrong & Co., of Elswick Works, Newcastle-on-Tyne for the supply of hydraulic machinery for the High-Level Coal Railway was accepted. The line was completed in 1856 and the first shipment of coal was made on 23rd December of that year. The capacity of the cranes provided was 4,000 tons per 12-hour day. Both box and ordinary wagons were handled, hauled by horse teams between Sandhills and the coal tips.

In March 1859, Messrs Whitford & Co., asked permission for coal cranes to be used for loading block ice into railway wagons. Permission was granted, at five pence per ton. Such practice was short-lived however.

In 1880 the L & Y Railway Company decided to double their line from Sandhills to the docks, so the Mersey Docks & Harbour Board resolved to extend the High-Level Coal Railway along the north side of Bramley-Moore Dock. A tender for the erection of the extension by Tees-side Engine & Engineering Works was accepted. A 280 h.p. compound pumping engine was supplied by Sir W. G. Armstrong of Newcastle-on-Tyne. The extension was built during 1881-2. In 1886 the old portion of the High-Level Railway was relaid with steel rails in place of the iron rails previously used.

The supremely ugly iron lifting bridge over Regent Road on which an ex-L & Y "pug" engine can usually be seen shunting the coal wagons, was made a fixed bridge in 1940. The line also crosses the Liverpool Overhead Railway (opened in 1893) by an iron fixed bridge, but the overhead line has to come down to street level in order to pass under this bridge. Until 1926 the Overhead Company's power station was situated here and its coal bunkers were supplied directly from the High-Level Coal Railway.

Upon the introduction of steam locomotives on the dock lines, the old Wellington Dock section of the High-Level line had to be relaid

26

with steel rails, as the original iron rails were well-worn and too light for locomotives.

Bramley-Moore Dock and the adjoining Wellington Dock were opened in 1844, being named after a former chairman of the Docks Committee and the "Iron Duke" respectively. Railway lines are literally "all over the place" in this locality, with a double track connection from the North Docks goods station to the docks railway crossing Regent Road, this connection dating from September 1858. In addition to the lines across Boundary Street, others cross Blackstone Street on the level. The approach lines to North Docks station and Bramley-Moore coal tips also pass above Boundary and Blackstone Streets on iron bridges of supremely ugly visage.

In Boundary Street at its south corner, at the junction with Regent Road, almost hidden out of site there is a small yard and workshop in which repairs to railway wagons are carried out. It is reached by a line from North Docks station that crosses the street on the level.

Proceeding onwards along Regent Road we next cross Fulton Street which makes make a sharp turn northwards and runs on to intersect Boundary Street. The high-level coal line crosses Fulton Street via a brick arch bridge amid industrial premises of various kinds. A few moments walking alongside the west wall of North Docks goods station, the intersection of Walter Street and Regent Road is reached, opposite the North Quay of Collingwood Dock, in an area of old industrial buildings and some of the more ancient docks. On the south side of narrow Walter Street stands the large Stanley Dock North warehouse, which was designed by Jesse Hartley and built in 1848. This building is surrounded by massive, high stone walls, and through a gateway in Regent Road runs a single-line branch from the dockside railway which passes along the north side of the warehouse in a narrow canyon-like situation formed by the building itself and the close-by high wall. This spur is connected with North Docks goods station by a single line across Walter Street laid in June 1855, which emerges from a gateway and enters another on the opposite side. The warehouse has arched openings ranged along the quayside, the arches being sprung from massive cast-iron columns. Between the warehouse and the wall alongside Regent Road stands a tall, castellated tower in grey stone, also a red-brick chimney belonging to a hydraulic power station. The tower was the work of Jesse Hartley in his usual "fairy-tale" castle style.

Immediately ahead now is the entrance/exit passage of Stanley Dock which is unique in that it is situated on the east side of the dock road (all the other docks are on the west side). The dock was named after the Chief Engineer of the Leeds-Liverpool Canal. From this dock a flight of five locks provide a connection between the River Mersey and the canal. The dock, and also the locks were opened in August 1848. The dock passage is spanned by a steel lifting bridge which carries the main dock road across. The docks railway shares, together with the Liverpool Overhead Railway, a separate double-decked steel swing bridge which is of more than usual interest in that the lower deck is arranged as a lifting bridge with two leaves, which can be raised to permit the passage of small vessels without interupting traffic on the Overhead Railway which uses the top deck. Before the construction of the overhead line, the docks railway crossed the Stanley passage by a single-deck swing bridge and so did the adjacent road on a separate bridge. At first single track was laid over the bridge but it was doubled in 1877. All traffic was stopped for ten days while this old bridge was replaced by the present structure upon construction of the Liverpool Overhead Railway.

Looking towards the river frontage a rather quaint structure meets the eye in the shape of a tall castellated tower which looks as though it is part of a fortress! This is the notable "Victoria Tower" which was designed by Jesse Hartley and built in 1848, this date being cut into the granite of which it is built. Formerly accompanied by other buildings of the period, including hydraulic installations, the tower now stands in solitary, stately isolation as all else was either destroyed in the blitz or demolished to make way for alterations. A particular feature of the tower, which is at the north-west corner of Salisbury Dock, is that it has six sides, with a large clock on each, so the time can be ascertained from any direction on land or river.

After crossing the lifting bridge via the planked footway that runs on the outside of the main girders, another notable building is reached — the enormous Stanley Tobacco Warehouse which was completed in 1900. This immense 14-storey building, into the construction of which 27,000,000 bricks were swallowed is a masterpiece of neat architecture and building skill. It is 125 feet high and 730 feet in length. Before this giant of a warehouse was built, the land on which it stands was made up by filling-in part of the dock, and so separated the Stanley north and south warehouses.

The tobacco warehouse was without direct rail access until 1931, when a branch was laid from the docks main line, crossing Regent Road and passing through a gateway in the fortress-like walls and running in a "canyon" along the south avenue between the tobacco warehouse and the Stanley south warehouse. Both these buildings stretch the full length of Saltney Street which runs from Great Howard Street to the dock road at the southern end of these buildings.

Before the Stanley tobacco warehouse was built the inland dock was of greater width than it is today. The older warehouses occupied the north and south quays and were rail-served from the beginning. A single-line spur from the dockside main line curved north-eastwards across Regent Road and passed through a gateway, and then ran inside the high wall separating the warehouse from Walter Street. A second line parallelled it alongside the warehouse but connection betweeen the two tracks was made via turntables, one of them connecting with the previously mentioned single line across Walter Street. The spur ran right round the perimeter of the dock as a single line, the situation on the south side being exactly the same as on the north side — two parallel lines linked by turntables. All the turntables gave access to the interior of the warehouse buildings. There was no dock railway connection on the south side however, the lines terminating inside the walls. The turntables were manufactured by the Bank Hall Foundry in 1855. Apparently all the rails on the south side were removed when the tobacco warehouse was built, as it was placed immediately adjacent to the South Stanley warehouse, covering the original dock quay and extending over what had previously been water.

Almost opposite the foot of Saltney Street is the Clarence Dock Overhead Railway station and behind it the Clarence Graving Dock, all that is left of the Clarence group of docks which were opened in 1830 by the Duke of Clarence. The main "wet" dock was filled in a century later to provide space for an electric power station, which will be referred to again shortly.

Clarence Dock occupies the site of the "Mile House Rocks" on which some ships met their doom in earlier times. Fishermen's cottages stood near the shore-line in the days before dock construction reached this area. Although the dock road was being extended in the early 1830's, it was through fields and sand dunes, whilst there was a fortress on the riverward side and bowling greens on what is now the site of North Docks goods station. On the south side of Clarence lies Trafalgar Dock, which was opened in 1836 and like most of the other very old docks has seen subsequent modernisation.

The next object to claim attention and an extremely large one at that, is the great Clarence Dock Power Station, with its tall, gaunt concrete chimneys which are referred to locally as the "ugly sisters". This power station was opened in 1931, having been built on the site of the former Clarence wet Dock. The enormous supplies of coal required to produce the volts are transported in 20-ton steel hopper wagons in trainloads from collieries in South Lancashire, and from as far afield as Killamarsh, near Sheffield. These trains enter the dock estate at Canada and Huskisson, and then travel along the dockside railway to and from Clarence. Two steam locomotives are in use at the power station, both owned by the Corporation Electricity Department, and these are continuously employed shunting hopper wagons between the dock road and the immense coal storage well with its huge grab-crane. It is a fascinating sight to watch one of the MD & HB 0-6-0 Saddle Tank engines hauling a coal train slogging slowly along with fierce exhaust, and bell tolling, the steel hoppers rumbling along behind it with a sound like distant thunder. These vehicles are fitted with extra-long coupling links so that a locomotive can pick them up in one-at-a-time fashion and so get the train on the move easier than would be the case if the whole train had to be started from rest with the engine taking the full weight at once. the long couplings also allow a train to negotiate sharp curves without buffer-locking. The results of a rough start with a train of hoppers can be quite exciting as the wagons are jerked into motion with the rumble of drawbars and clashing of buffers creating a noisy accompaniment, whilst black clouds of coal dust drift off the loads! The grunting and shrieking of wheel flanges on sharp curves is another characteristic of these hopper wagons when moving along the grooved rails of the dock road.

During, and following for a while World War 2, some coal for Clarence power station came in coastal ships and had to be unloaded into railway wagons at Nelson Dock and then hauled to Clarence. To carry this coal the Liverpool Corporation Electricity Department aquired a number of North Eastern Railway design wooden hopper wagons from the L & NER company, of a type seen normally only in the North East around Newcastle-on-Tyne, Gateshead etc. They looked quite strange and out of place on Liverpool docks.

After passing Trafalgar Branch Dock and Victoria Dock, both opened in 1836, another large railway installation is reached. This is Waterloo goods station, which was built by the London & North Western Railway Company as long ago as 1849, and subsequently enlarged and extended., Here, Braithwaite Poole of Hoylake Railway fame was Goods Manager long ago. Although it is opposite Victoria Dock, the station and yards situated at the end of a branch from Edge Hill, are named Waterloo because here the main dock highway is entitled Waterloo Road, Waterloo Dock being a little further south. The premises extend in width from Oil Street to Formby Street and in its prime Waterloo station was a busy place indeed. It was heavily hammered during the air raids of 1940-41 but was extensively patched up and partly rebuilt soon afterwards. Oil Street was named after the oil mill of Messrs Earles & Carter which was demolished to make way for extensions to the goods depot.

A double line in grooved rails curving across Waterloo Road in a northerly direction connects the north section of the huge and gloomy depot with the docks main line, this connection dating from 1858. Further south is a single line crossing, also in grooved rails, that takes the long branch from Edge Hill via Victoria and Waterloo tunnels onto the dock estate so that passenger trains can reach the Riverside station, of which more later. To our right are the two enormous Waterloo corn warehouses, designed by G. F. Lyster and built in 1867 — massive stone and brick buildings with rows of colonaded arches at roadway level. They lie parallel to the River Mersey, and the bombed remains of a third such building, transverse to the others is at the north end of the Waterloo Dock, which itself lies between the two main warehouses which are identical in size and design. On the left, extending from Formby Street to Paisley Street loom the high mills and warehouses of Messrs. J. Bibby & Sons, that spread over Neptune, Dundee, Barton and Galton Streets, these narrow thoroughfares resembling dark canyons between the high buildings and warehouses of various vintages and styles. There was once a windmill at the foot of Formby Street, which was converted into a tavern, appropriately named "The Rotunda". This vanished when the mills were extended early in the present century.

In May 1915 the MD & HB agreed to lay a siding into Formby Street to serve Bibby's premises, and a set of points was inserted into the docks main line for the purpose. It would appear however that the siding was not put in, but the points remained in position (they were still in place when the dockside railway closed).

On this section of the dock road a massive stone wall separates the dock estate from the public roadway, and within the walls several parallel sets of rails run for some distance. Firstly, there are the Up and Down main lines of the MD & HB railway, next the Riverside line, then two long sidings that serve the east side of the corn warehouse. Tracks once ran through this building and the pattern of the stone setts show where they formerly existed. Rails also crossed a long-vanished swing bridge across Waterloo Dock passage here.

Beyond Roberts Street the dock road curves in a south-easterly direction and becomes Bath Street, lined by ancient warehouses, some dating back to the 1830's and various industrial premises, stores catering for shipping and so on. To the right is the dock wall, with various gateways each with its stonework police hut, and behind it the lengthy expanse of Princes Dock, originally opened in July 1821 (the Coronation day of King George IV). The first ship to enter was the "May" — a Liverpool-built West Indiaman. An old fort, built in 1777 once stood at the foot of Dutton Street but this was demolished and the land included in the dock area. Princes Dock station of the Overhead Railway is opposite the foot of Roberts Street. The dock road is quite narrow in this locality, the flow of traffic not being rendered any easier by the lines of parked vehicles waiting to get into the docks. Included in the line-up are horse-drawn carts and steam wagons, but mostly, they are motor lorries from places near and far, the diesel and petrol engines now having largely displaced horse and steam power, though a surprising number of horses still plod along the dock road.

Riverside station, just mentioned, was built because there long existed a lack of convenient train-to-ship connections at Liverpool. Passengers for ocean ships arriving at Lime Street station, were conveyed to the landing stage in horse-drawn omnibuses and, of course, their baggage also had to be transported — the reverse was the case for disembarking passengers. The steamship companies were not content with this state of affairs which just continued with no improvement until one company, the Inman Line, transferred their ships to Southampton and the possibility existed that others might do likewise. This move soon resulted in some action, and a site for a station at the landing stage was made available on the west side of Princes Dock, construction commencing in December 1894.

Riverside station, built and owned by the Mersey Docks & Harbour Board has two platforms, each 790 feet in length. It was opened 12th June 1895. The first train to arrive was a special one from Stafford with carriages from the 9.00 am ex-London (Euston) conveying passengers for America via the White Star liner "Germanic". The train was hauled by one of the L & NW 0-6-0 Special Saddle Tank engines on the last stage of its journey through the long tunnel from Edge Hill to Waterloo dock, and on to Riverside via the docks railway.

Liverpool was, of course, a major passenger port for many years, with ocean liner sailings almost every day, and for many years too, Riverside station was a busy and interesting place. Its platforms were walked upon by the elite of the world — millionaires, magnates, tycoons, film and stage stars, and the glamour of feminine society — a place to see the latest fashions from both the old and new worlds. At the other end of the scale there were the less fortunate steerage passengers, and the emigrants who did not travel in luxury. In two wars millions of troops passed through Riverside station — in the last conflict 4,648 special trains conveyed a total of 1,747,505 servicemen to and from the station, including USA forces.

The personnel from North America, accustomed to enormous locomotives, high-capacity freight cars and capacious passenger coaches noted with astonishment the much smaller British trains, and were quite impressed with the degree of comfort which our railways accomplished within the restricted constructional limits imposed by the British loading gauge. Of course, at that time, main line locomotives could not work through to Riverside, and the engines the Americans saw first were the small and ancient ex-L & NWR 0-6-2 Coal Tanks, and naturally they thought that these were going to haul the train the whole way to their destination! They knew nothing of course, of the impending engine-change at Edge Hill, but even our largest locomotives were small in comparison with those of the USA, and caused much surprise.

Riverside station has always been well kept — painted frequently and cleaned often, presenting a smart appearance. Indeed, even the sleepers and track ballast look as though they are regularly cleaned! Few Liverpool citizens seem to be aware of this railway station so close to the famous landing stage over which millions of people pass annually.

Elaborate precautions are taken with the working of the boat trains to and from Riverside as, not only do they have to cross the busy, heavily-trafficked main dock road, but also the double track of the docks main line within the dock walls, and then along the roadway past a busy corn warehouse with rail and lorry traffic before curving to cross the waterway connection between Princes and Waterloo Docks via a swing bridge at which a small signal box is situated — there is another box at Riverside station. Single line working by Pilotman is practised and signals for the Riverside line are interlocked with semaphore signals on the docks railway, (the only ones on that system) so that no goods trains can approach the main-line crossing while a passenger train is being worked. A flagman walks ahead of the train as it proceeds along at walking pace to warn of the train's approach, just like on that first journey on the Stockton & Darlington Railway in 1825, except that the flagman on that occasion rode on a horse! Incidentally, the operating wires for the MD & HB signals which are of the lower-quadrant type, are carried along the top of the high dock wall.

For many years there was a double-track approach to Riverside, whilst there were also several sharp curves and a swing bridge that had weight restrictions so that only small locomotives could be used to haul the passenger trains. In L & NW days two particular locomotives were kept for the work, these being a couple of the famous Special Saddle Tank class designed by John Ramsbottom, but unlike the remainder of the class these two had square tanks. The engines were L & NW No. 3186 which was named "Euston" and No. 3021 which carried the name "Liverpool". They were equipped with condensing apparatus to reduce the amount of exhaust emitted into the tunnels. Other engines such as the ordinary 0-6-0 Special Tank and sometimes a Bissell Truck 0-4-2 Tank were employed when traffic was heavy, entailing the provision of extra trains or when either "Euston", "Liverpool", or both were out of service. For most of the life of the Riverside line however, right up to 1950, the 0-6-2 Coal Side Tank engines were used on the passenger trains, in two's or three's depending on the weight of a train. The main-line locomotive that had brought the train in was detached at Edge Hill and replaced by the tunnel engines, the reverse procedure applying to Up trains.

In order to complete the Riverside station story we will come forward to more recent events, and resume this 1946 survey a little further on. The inconvenience of being obliged to change engines at Edge Hill, plus the restrictions imposed by the sharp curves and swing bridge at Princes Dock were tolerated for no less than 54 years, but at long last, plans for replacing the bridge by a stonger structure and easing-out of the curves were made, in 1949, and scheduled to commence in November of that year, and to be completed by March 1950. Riverside station was to be closed while the work was in progress. Buses and vans were to be used for passengers and baggage between Lime Street station and the landing stage. In October 1949 however, a ship collided with the swing bridge and put it out of action, trapping two complete trains and four Coal Tank engines on the wrong side. Nevertheless, it was found possible to get these over the bridge the next day, whereupon it was decided to commence the work planned for the following month there and then.

Completion of the aforementioned works enabled main-line locomotives to be used throughout and the ancient Coal Tanks were at last displaced on the boat train workings. The leading express types were henceforward employed, such as Royal Scot, Jubilee, and Patriot 4-6-0's of the former LMS, also the BR Standard Britannia Class 4-6-2's. Empty carriage workings were shared between ex-L & NW 0-8-0, ex-LMS 8F 2-8-0 and Class 5 4-6-0 classes. Latterly main-line diesel-electric locomotives were employed on both through train and empty workings, whilst on one occasion at least, a diesel multiple-unit train visited Riverside station on a special excursion for a local railway society.

It was a rare experience in Britain to stand on a busy main road amid teeming motor traffic and witness the sight of a main-line passenger train, with its occupants leaning from the carriage windows, wondering were on earth they were going as the train emerged from the tunnel, passed under several bridges, with tall warehouses and steaming mills on either side, crossed the road while policemen held up the traffic, and then proceeded slowly along the stone-setted roadway running on tramway-type grooved rails among road vehicles, to eventually come across ships moored in Waterloo and Princes Docks. It was always fascinating to reflect that a short while earlier the same train had been rushing headlong over a busy fully signalled main line, and after the completion of the London-Liverpool electrification had probably been streaking along at 100 miles per hour! Now-it was travelling at walking pace with a flagman striding ahead! The ritual of changing engines at Edge Hill, which was abolished in 1950 when the improvements were completed, was reintroduced after electrification, the electric locomotive that had brought the train from London, being replaced by a steam or diesel locomotive, the reverse happening for trains from Riverside to London and elsewhere.

In the year 1953 some of the Boat trains were given names "Empress Voyager" for that running in connection with Canadian Pacific ships. Later, some Class 40 diesel-electric locomotives were named after well-known liners.

Although the vast majority of trains that used Riverside station were to or from London, in latter years trains were run also to and from other places. Some services were operated in connection with the Isle of Man steamers, mainly excursions from inland towns to the island, some of these trains returning in the small hours of the morning.

By the late 1950's the days of Liverpool as a passenger port were numbered and business was declining. For years aircraft had been eroding overseas passenger traffic and one by one the great ocean liners departed from Liverpool until only Canadian Pacific and Elder Dempster remained, and where once trains ran almost every day the traffic dropped to one or two trains a week or even less, so the writing appeared on the wall for Riverside. Rumours of closure circulated for a long time but the end came on Thursday, 25th February 1971 when the last train, a troop special carrying soldiers returning from Ulster, departed. It was hauled by an English-Electric Class 40 diesel-electric locomotive, and after the train had crossed the main dock road, the gates were closed behind it and so ended a useful and fascinating operation after 76 years. Thereafter for a year or two, passenger ships calling at the landing stage (cruise liners only) had no train waiting alongside — the position had reverted to that which prevailed before 1895, buses, taxis and vans taking passengers and their baggage between the stage and Lime Street station. Nowadays the few cruise ships to and from Liverpool moor in the docks and not at the landing stage.

During the 1930's Princes Dock was widened on the west side and this work necessitated singling of the Riverside station track on the west side of the swing bridge. At the same time cattle sidings that served a jetty on the river front were abolished. The points and some remnants of the very old track forming these sidings were still in position well into the 1970's.

In 1882, before Riverside station was built, the London & North Western Company sought permission from the Dock Board to run passenger trains to Princes Dock along the docks railway line from Alexandra Dock, which they would reach via the Edge Hill-Bootle Branch. Permission was granted so long as the carriages were hauled by horses! It is not surprising that the service did not materialise. The toll was to be one shilling per carriage for use of the dockside rails.

The L & NWR had the monopoly of the Riverside traffic but amazingly the Midland Railway Company ran an experimental passenger train from Brunswick Dock to Riverside soon after the station was opened. This train encountered so many hold-ups on the busy dock road that the experiment proved a failure. The idea was to run through trains between London (St. Pancras) and Riverside in competition with the L & NWR.

Having digressed somewhat from our 1946 survey in looking into the fate of Riverside station, we now resume our observation of things as they used to be. Proceeding along the dock road, we must take great care when encountering the heavy lorries passing to and from the extensive range of buildings that comprise the soap and seed mills. As the road takes a slight curve to the left the twin towers of the Royal Liver building at the Pier Head and other commercial buildings appear in the near distance. On the right-hand side behind the fortress-like wall is the Princes Dock locomotive shed (built in 1906) and the repair shop (built in 1941) of the Mersey Docks & Harbour Board railway system. There is little of railway interest to be seen from the road hereabouts as the lines are behind the dock wall, but the omnipresent Overhead Railway still accompanies the dock road, a train passing every few minutes. The road becomes quite narrow here, lined on its East side with warehouses and other buildings, most of them being very old. Indeed, one warehouse at the corner of Roberts Street was built as long ago as 1834. Presently the visitor reaches King Edward Street, which trails into the dock road at an angle. From Roberts Street to this junction the dock road is named Bath Street, whilst from King Edward Street as far as the junction with Chapel Street it is called New Quay.

The quaintly-named warehouse-lined street called Lancelot's Hey diverges to the left at an angle a short distance beyond the King Edward Street junction. All the warehouses in the "Hey" are ancient, though in earlier times it was partly a residential street. Next for attention is one of the finest and most imposing ranges of warehouses in Liverpool, situated on the east side of New Quay. They rise to a considerable height, and being constructed of red bricks and yellow sandstone, are impressive and pleasing in design. There is no pavement in front of these warehouses and rows of lorries being loaded or unloaded make it advisable to cross over to the opposite side of the road. Immediately before reaching Chapel Street which joins New Quay on the East side there is the entrance/exit of the Mersey Road tunnel, opened in 1934. Previous to the construction of the tunnel, the land on which the portal is situated was occupied by warehouses and a pub. The Liverpool Parish Church of St. Nicholas, with its tower crowned by a gleaming gilt model of an old-time sailing ship, stands on the South corner of Chapel Street, an oasis of peace in a whirlpool of commercial activity. Standing next to the church is the Tower Building which replaced an earlier block of the same name in 1907. The old Tower Building, completed in 1856 occupied the site of the ancient Tower of Liverpool which dated from 1252, and was used for many years as a prison of evil repute. We are on historic ground here!

In order to keep as near to the river as possible one must cross over to the west side of the dock road near the gates of Princes Dock, through which the rails of the MD & HB railway emerge to run along the street still beneath the structure of the Overhead Railway however. On the right is the famous floating roadway, the pontoon bridge built in 1873 that takes vehicles onto the landing stage. The area is dominated by the three great Pier Head buildings — Royal Liver, Cunard and Dock offices which stand side-by-side — three widely-differing styles of architecture to make for variety and interest. They stand on the site of the old Georges Dock, which was opened in 1771 but reconstructed and enlarged in 1822-1825.

On the east side of the dock a vast range of warehouses was built in 1793, with colonaded footwalks at ground level, which were named "Goree Piazzas". These warehouses had become dilapidated and dingy by the time of World War II, only the ground floors being used as shops, stores or restaurants. Renovation was not likely, due not only to the enormous cost but also due to the fact that the buildings served no useful purpose after the Georges Dock was filled-in, which took place after the water was drained out in July 1900. The blitz of 1940-41 caused such extensive damage to the Goree Piazzas that complete demolition was the only practical course to be followed, and much of this was done during the war. Remnants of the buildings survived for some years after the end of the war however. The disappearance of the enormous warehouses made a profound difference to the dock road scene in this locality, creating a wide open space out of what was formerly a dark canyon into which the sun penetrated briefly around mid-day.

Before the turn of the century, ships sailing to and from the West Indies, Brazil, Canada, Africa, Australia, North America, Baltic, European and Mediterranean ports could be seen moored in Georges Dock, along the east side of which were long, single storey sheds, the docks railway running between these and the main road. Until 1886 a pedestrian bridge connecting St. Nicholas's Churchyard and St. Nicholas Place passed over the dock road and railway, whilst horse-drawn vehicles crossed the bridge leading to the Pier Head at St. Nicholas's Place in days before the floating bridge, linking the landing stage to the roadway closed the passage between Princes and Georges Docks. Such vehicles including trams and omnibuses also crossed the swing bridge leading to Mann Island at the foot of James Street. The land on the west side of Georges Dock, now the Pier Head, was reclaimed from the river, being made up by tipping of stone and rubbish. Once the river lapped the walls of St. Nicholas's Church, the original shoreline being marked today by the street called The Strand, so that even the dock road is on made-up land.

The track used by the horse trams consisted of centre-grooved rail, the car wheels having a central flange on the tyre, and the intersection of these rails with those of the docks railway resulted in some interesting crossing-work. For many years horse-drawn trams met horse-drawn trains at this location, before steam locomotives were brought into use on the dock lines.

The first major change in the Pier Head area was the construction of the Overhead Railway, opened in 1893, and the building of the Pier Head station on that line. For a few years electric trains ran overhead whilst all the road traffic below was horse-drawn except for steam wagons and traction engines. After Georges Dock was filled-in, the great domed Dock Office building was erected and completed in 1903, followed by the Royal Liver Building completed in 1909, and next the Cunard Building, opened in 1914. The Mersey Tunnel Ventilating building nearby was completed in 1934. It is of interest to note that although the Georges Dock vanished early in the century the stretch of dock road adjacent to the Royal Liver Building is still named Georges Dock Gates.

Electric trams began to run to the Pier Head, in 1900 in company with horse trams, but the older vehicles had vanished by 1903, and as the century progressed, motor cars and lorries began to appear in ever-increasing numbers, though it was very many years before the giant draught horses finally disappeared from the dock road. Horse-drawn lorries still clatter past laden with bales of cotton or other freight as we survey the scene in this fascinating district, but they become fewer as time passes and will soon vanish completely.

From time to time goods trains pass the Pier Head. They are hauled by the ex-L & Y "Pug" Tank or the MD & HB Saddle Tank engines. The trains travel slowly along, beneath the Overhead Railway. A flagman alights from the engine to hold up traffic on the main intersections as the train crosses. This archaic rule still persists, for presumably a train is considered to be dangerous — even travelling at walking pace, but motor vehicles pass across at speeds which individual drivers choose, often with scant attention to safety, but the trains are strictly governed by ancient regulations. The installation of traffic signals in recent times has cut down much of the speeding-through of road vehicles however. Actually, until 1932, a flagman was obliged to walk ahead of every train along the full length of the docks railway whilst additional warning was, and still is, given by the ever-tolling bell worked by a rocker on the engine's motion. Occasionally a blast on the whistle is necessary to warn someone about to park a car or lorry on the track (especially was this so after removal of the Overhead Railway and people thought that the docks railway was part of the abandoned city tramways). Trains on the dock road are limited to 19 wagons during the day but can be made up to 31 by night, which is after 10.00 pm. Most drivers of road vehicles are not amused when their headlong progress is halted for a couple of minutes while a train crosses their path!

In addition to the trio of large buildings here, there is the fine White Star Line building on the corner of James Street, and it is worthwhile pausing here for a few moments to observe the scene, for to anyone interested in transport this is a veritable Mecca. Here can be seen the Overhead Railway, electric trams, buses, cars, lorries, horse-drawn vehicles, steam lorries and other road vehicles, also steam freight trains, ships and perhaps an aeroplane flying above whilst just a little way along James Street is the Mersey underground railway station. On the south-west corner of Mann Island stands the tall brick pumping station of the Mersey Railway, in which powerful pumps clear water from the tunnel — a continuous task.

Here, in 1946, we know nothing of the changes about to come which will render this intensely fascinating locality devoid of almost every vestige of interest — everything seems to have a future at the moment, though the tramways are threatened, an unfortunate prospect because up to now the system has been partially modernised, though intensive wartime use has taken its toll. No abandonment of tram routes took place until June, 1948 however.

Mann Island, on the right *was* indeed an island when Georges Dock existed, as it was reached only by bridges from the mainland. The site on which now stands the large Voss garage and motor showroom was, until circa 1929 occupied by ancient buildings of a motly variety — small shops, tea rooms, stores, warehouses, pubs and a few dwellings, whilst at the riverward end was Manchester Dock and the Great Western Railway yard. The latter had no rail connection, goods being ferried to and fro across the Mersey in barges, and when the Mersey Tunnel was completed, in motor lorries, though some of the latter used the river vehicle ferries before the tunnel was built.

Not only has the GWR a depot at Mann Island — others are located at Langton Dock, Lightbody Street and Chaloner Street. The company also has an office in nearby James Street. The GWR tried to reach Liverpool for years, but failed to do so and had to content itself with off-line offices and depots served by barges, horse-drawn carts, and later by motor vehicles. It was always pleasant to see their chocolate and cream-liveried vehicles in Liverpool's streets and read that wonderful title — GREAT WESTERN!

Before moving on from this most fascinating area, a study of the tramway-railway crossings is of interest. There are three such crossings in the locality, at St. Nicholas Place, Water Street and James Street. The crossings are made from tough manganese steel in order to stand up to the tremendous hammering they receive from the wheels of the hundreds of trams that pass over them daily, these wheels setting up a merry clatter as they encounter the gaps provided for the wheels of railway vehicles. The crossing units are, of course, formed of two different dimensions of rail though both are of grooved tramway pattern, but the groove and running surface are narrower on the tram section than those on the railway portion, the latter which have to accommodate wheels with larger flanges and tread. All the tracks are paved with granite setts.

Immediately south of the Mann Island intersection James Street "Overhead" station overlooks the busy roadways and the bombed remains of the Harbour Master's house immediately below it, which nestled between the Overhead Railway structure and the Mersey Railway Pumping Station. Two streets leading from Mann Island, Irwell Street and Nova Scotia, lead to the site of the former

Manchester Dock, which was used by small vessels and barges. The dock was built piecemeal fashion between 1772 and 1806, being later extended and provided with gates. It was leased to the Mersey & Irwell Navigation Company, then to the Trustees of the Duke of Bridgewater, but in 1851 the Dock Trustees purchased it. The dock passed into the control of the Mersey Docks & Harbour Board when that organisation was formed in 1858. It was next leased jointly to the London & North Western and Great Western Railway Companies in 1872, who used it for barges conveying merchandise to and from Birkenhead. The lease ended in 1922 but the dock was again leased to the GWR which had its goods depot on Mann Island., The dock was filled-in with spoil from the Mersey road tunnel excavations during 1928, though the railway company retained the site as a road motor depot.

Continuing along Strand Street, as this section of the dock road is called, Sea Brow will be noticed — a narrow street following the same "line" as The Strand, and marking the site of the original Mersey shore before the landmaking works were carried out. Strand Street is lined on its east side by very old buildings that serve a variety of dockland purposes. On the west side lies Canning Dock, which was developed from three graving docks that Thomas Steers built in connection with an outer harbour which he provided for his famous Old Dock made from the Pool. The largest of the graving docks was originally associated with Salthouse Dock, the next one southwards, but was converted to a "wet" dock and the outer harbour altered in 1829. The aforementioned "wet" dock that was formed as a result of these works was named Canning, after the famous statesman. A number of modifications have been carried out since the dock was built, but it still presents an old-world look with its ancient sheds and sandstone quays. On the north side of the dock an ancient crane stands on the quayside and a single-line branch leaves the Down line of the docks railway, curving westwards onto the quay and becoming a loop so that an engine could get out at the far end after hauling wagons onto the quayside. This siding was laid in 1866. The track here is of the ancient double-rail type, the short-bladed points containing a great deal of ironmongery! No train has used the loop since at least circa 1936, as general cargo traffic ebbed away from this part of the dock long ago. Until 1938 steam fishing trawlers unloaded their catches here and since then the quay has been little used, though other parts of the dock are still visited by Irish cargo ships and a few coasting vessels, otherwise there is little commerce left in the immediate area, the docks being obsolete and too small for modern traffic.

The area surrounding Canning Place is the oldest and most romantic part of the Liverpool docks system, and is quite picturesque in its own peculiar way, where everything is of ancient vintage like a set from an historical play or film. This is a favourite venue for artists — men, and women too, who love to paint the dockland scene, especially the view looking northwards from the south end of Canning Dock with its vista of the Pier Head buildings beyond the still waters of the old dock itself. Atkinson Grimshaw painted some of his "dock road by moonlight" scenes here in the 1890's, two of which can be seen in the Walker Art Gallery, but many others have recorded the scene on canvas in recent years, and there is scarcely an art exhibition held in the city that does not include several paintings of this quarter. Painting on the busy north docks would prove to be a harrassing task, except perhaps on Saturday afternoons, and Sundays, when traffic has quietened down, but apart from the side nearest the dock road, Canning is quite peaceful even on weekdays.

In days of long ago the scene which this district presented was a decidedly more squalid one than it is at the present time — it was the sailor's quarter with its lodging houses, ale houses, ships chandlers and other stores that met the needs of vessels and their crews. It was also a residential district, but not in the best sense of the word, for the people who inhabited it were mostly poverty-stricken and lived, grossly overcrowded, in dingy little dwellings in the narrow streets and courts. Few persons from outside the area ever ventured into it, even though the commercial centre and shops were but a stones-throw away. It was also a notorious "red light" district known as the "Devil's Acre" where press-gangs made their rounds and where Maggie May wandered, in her gown so fine as the old song says. The dockside venturer would encounter her and her numorous colleagues all along the dock road, and were as much a part of the scene as the sailors and dock workers. Time has mellowed the memory of the hard past, and has done likewise with the "judies" who were among the host of characters who have contributed to Liverpool's rich history.

Nowhere else along the docks is possessed of such an abundance of "atmosphere" and romance as the district around Canning Place with its time-worn decaying old buildings. The wartime blitz dealt severely with the locality, but a great deal remains and the old aura is not entirely lost. On looking across the expanse of old docks, one can well picture the scenes of other days when the district teemed with life and many ships were moored to the quayside bollards with sails furled, their tall masts and spars forming complex patterns, or those same vessels being towed into or out of the docks by steam tugs with churning paddle wheels and black smoke pouring from tall, slim funnels. Here too, in imagination, you can hear the ghostly echoes of the shanties sung by the hard-working crews as they rythmically performed the arduous tasks demanded by those well-loved ships of long ago. In reality however, all you hear today is the sea wind sighing around the venerable buildings of this historic quarter which lies so close to the shopping and commercial centre of the city, yet worlds apart from it in character.

Canning Place, the "centre" of this district is a very large square, in the middle of which the famous Custom House was situated, but this is now a forlorn heap of ruins, as it was an early casualty of the wartime blitz. The old building with its great central dome and pillared entrances was one of the sights of Liverpool in its day. Custom House station on the Overhead Railway is on the west side of Canning Place. On the right, a wide cobblestoned roadway in which is embedded a sinlge line of railway (formed of separate rails and check rails) leads to a swing bridge, and beyond this structure lies the famous Albert Dock, the great warehouses of which dominate the view to the west.

Albert Dock occupies the site of former shipbuilding yards. It was designed by Jesse Hartley, as a self-contained dock and warehouse complex — a large, square water area completely surrounded by huge warehouses so that goods could be placed in store direct from the ships without having to be carted some distance, as is the case at other docks. The Albert Dock and its associated buildings took five years to complete, the work commencing in 1840 and finished in 1845. The dock was opened by Prince Albert, the Prince Consort, after whom it was named. The warehouses are constructed entirely in bricks and iron, their inner faces, on the quaysides having at their lower extremities, great semi-elliptical arches resting upon massive cast-iron columns, whilst quaint hydraulic cranes line the quays. Over the years Albert Dock has hardly changed, and it is quite easy to imagine tea clippers from China and East Indiamen moored at the ancient quays instead of the steamers and motor ships of the middle 20th century. To walk beneath the colonades is an experience not to be missed, for you step back into history and are inspired with awe at the magnitude of the work involved in building this unique dock, so different from every other in the port of Liverpool. An ornate clock tower surmounts one of the warehouses, themselves of ultra-simple design but highly functional, and even picturesque in their own way. They were however, condemned by Picton in his "Memorials of Liverpool" as bleak expanses of naked brickwork!

Facing the observer looking towards Albert Dock, is the Dock Traffic office. This is fronted by a grand columned portico made entirely in cast-iron, which was designed by Philip Hardwick (who also designed the great Doric portico at Euston station in London). The single railway line which branches from the "main line" opposite Canning Place is still in the ancient rail and check-rail form, laid in large granite setts and cobblestones. This line crosses the swing bridge over the Canning-Salthouse passage, after which it branches into two, the left-hand track entering the most northerly warehouse by an end doorway, and passes out again further along to join the line outside the warehouse along its north wall. A wagon turntable at the east end of the warehouse gave access to a short side-bay, but this turntable has been removed. The south quay of Canning Dock is dominated by tall hoppers and grab cranes for sand and gravel which are dredged from the river bed and unloaded here, being used for building purposes. A fleet of steam coasters with tall black funnels bring the material into the dock, after which motor trucks carry it away to various building sites.

A disused hydraulic pumping station, built in 1875, stands on the quayside nearby — an ornate red-brick building with a beautifully-designed brick chimney. The premises are now used by a firm of sail-makers. This is just one of several, now derelict, hydraulic installations along the Liverpool docks,

Adjoining Albert Dock on the east side is the Salthouse Dock, which was opened in 1753 and took its title from the salt works established here by the Blackburn family, of Hale, in about 1800. It was originally called the South Dock. In 1846 the main dock road, from Canning Place as far South as Sparling Street was re-aligned and Salthouse Dock enlarged. Between these two points the road is called Wapping. There are several items of interest along Wapping — firstly the ex-Lancashire & Yorkshire Railway company's Wapping & Salthouse goods stations, two separate buildings which are bisected by the narrow, industrial Ansdell Street. The building nearest to Canning Place was built in 1914 on a site formerly occupied by shops and business premises, and a single line of rails crosses Wapping at an angle to enter the shed, the points at which it leaves the main line being opposite the south side of Canning Place. The depot "next door" beyond Ansdell Street is older, having been opened in 1901, and like its neighbour, stands on the site of former shops and dockside business premises. There is a 'Y' connection with the MD & HB main line at the main gate of the goods shed at the corner of Salthouse Lane, and several times daily the diminutive ex-L & Y "Pug" Saddle Tank engines work-trains to and from these goods stations. The rather ornate but now shabby goods office building is on the corner of Ansdell Street and like the other buildings in this area has suffered from the ravages of time, wind and rain, whilst the wartime blitz took its toll, the large number of gaps in the surrounding buildings giving adequate testimony to the amount of pounding the district received.

Along the opposite (west) side of Wapping runs a very lengthy single-storey goods transit shed of ancient vintage, dated 1855, with walls of granite in a crazy-paving effect — more of Jesse Hartley's whimsicality! Behind this long shed is the narrow east quay of Salthouse Dock. The south end of this long dockside shed is at Gower Street, one of the few thoroughfare inside the dock estate to bear a name. This street runs between sheds and other buildings down to the river wall. A single line enters the long shed via a side door and emerges through an arched portal at the Gower Street end. Beyond the latter street a similar shed extends as far as Grayson Street and accommodates goods unloaded from ships moored at the east side of Wapping Basin, an extension to the dock which opened in 1858.

Inside the dock estate here, there are several items of very great interest, the largest and most noticeble being the Duke's Warehouse, built in 1811, serving Duke's Dock which was opened in 1773. The nobleman, after whom the dock was named, was the Duke of Bridgewater, of canal fame, who had the dock built as a terminal for vessels carrying goods to and from Manchester via the Bridgewater Canal which enters the River Mersey at Runcorn. The dock was constructed by James Brindley, the canal engineer. On the west side of Wapping Basin is Duke's Place, which was once part of a dockside street. A special feature of the Duke's Warehouse is the series of arches at the base through which water flows and allows barges to sail right inside for loading or unloading under cover. The area hereabouts is really "olde worlde" in complete contrast to the docks further south which, although they are old, are quite capacious. Unlike most of the north docks, they lie parellel to the River Mersey, though various branch docks are transversely situated.

The next water area reached is Wapping Dock, which is bounded, on the riverward side by King's Nos. 1 and 2 Docks. The original King's Docks were opened in 1788 but have been much-improved over the years, though reconstruction, which took place during 1852 involved narrowing of the original dock so that the Wapping Dock could be constructed, and this was opened in 1858.

On the east side of Wapping, Hurst Street diverges at an angle, and in the vee of the junction stands the "Baltic Fleet", a fine old dockland public house with a truly romantic seafaring name. On the west side of the dock road and stretching for some distance is the enormous Wapping Warehouse with its acres of brickwork, overlooking everything in the vicinity. This huge storehouse was designed by Jesse Hartley and its construction took from 1850 to 1857. Railway track was laid into the Wapping warehouse in 1857, with turntables giving access to interior loading bays, but the rail facilities were under-used and were removed about 1880. The positions in which the rails formerly existed can be discerned in the pattern of the sett paving.

At the north-east corner of the Wapping warehouse stands one of Jesse Hartley's conical grey stone watch towers with a crooked dagger design worked into the masonary in a quaint fairy-tale style which is quite astonishing to find in this dockland setting.

The Wapping warehouse was well hammered and set on fire during the blitz of late 1940, but is of such immense strength that it survived and part of the damaged areas were rebuilt. A large quantity of brickwork, blasted out by the bombing fell onto the docks railway and the bridge-work of the Overhead Railway, which pass alongside the east wall of the building.

A short length of rail, curving north to west from the docks line at the North end of the Wapping warehouse, is a remnant of the branch that was laid in 1865 to serve premises owned by the Trustees of the Duke of Bridgewater, but this line ceased to be used many years ago and most of it was removed. Its former course can be traced in places by observing the filled-in channels in the granite setts where the rails formerly existed.

At the southern extremity of the wapping warehouse the Overhead Railway had its Wapping Dock station, whilst on the opposite side of the dock road stand the extensive old buildings of Park Lane LMS goods station which occupies all the land between Sparling and Blundell Streets. This station originated in 1829-30 as the Wapping terminal of the pioneer Liverpool & Manchester Railway, and is the place at which the now extensive dockside railway had its beginnings, an extension of the L & M line into King's Dock to serve a coal yard being the first penetration of rails into the dock estate.

When the L & NWR depot was built, several streets and industrial buildings existed on the riverward side of Wapping. These were Ironmonger Lane, Wapping Lane, Willacy Place and Lower Sparling Street. A double line emerged from the L & NW yard passing directly across Wapping, through a warehouse, and on the other side a number of turntables enabled access to a dockside shed and along the quayside. There was also a coal yard here, owned by the London & North Western railway. All vanished during the dock reconstruction works of the 1850's.

A double-line branch, laid in grooved rail, curves south to east across Wapping, connecting Park Lane yard with the main docks railway. Here also, a double-track branch curves from the latter to serve the Queen's group of docks via a steel bowstring girder swing bridge. These particular docks originated with the old Queen's Dock which opened on 17th April 1796. This dock originally extended only to the foot of Greenland Street, but was extended southwards in 1816. It was again enlarged and rebuilt in 1856. The main dock lies parallel with the roadway, with two transverse branch docks and a graving dock on the riverward side. The railway runs onto the river wall in front of these docks and ends abruptly on a curve at the north corner of Queen's No. 1 Branch Dock. This line along the river wall, from which a spur runs to Queen's Graving Dock, was laid in 1923. It had been intended to continue the line along the side of the No. 1 Branch Dock, but this did not materialise, hence the dead-end. No buffers are provided — the rails simply end, like those at a tram terminus.

Before the present Queen's Branch docks were built, the area at the riverward side of the main dock consisted of several small inlets from the Mersey, and included a wharf called the Manchester Old Quay. A thoroughfare named Baffin Street ran parallel with the dock on its west side, but this vanished during the first phase of the alterations. Baffin Street was named after Baffin Island of whaling fame. The whaling industry once had a base in Liverpool, but is one of the vanished activities of the port, along with ship-building, which once flourished along these south docks during the 19th century, several shipyards having been obliterated by dock extensions etc.

From Park Lane goods depot as far as Parliament Street, the dock road is named Chaloner Street. On the left there are several lengthy streets that consist mainly of warehouses of various vintages, industrial premises, workshops and some dwelling houses also — Blundell Street, Kitchen Street, Bridgewater Street, Watkinson Street, Norfolk Street, Brick Street, Jordan Street, Greenland Street and Parliament Street — an interesting selection of names, a few with local significance. These streets, in the earlier years of the 19th century were a mixture of crowded slum dwellings, cramped courts, premises catering for seamens' needs and pleasures, public houses and warehouses of small dimensions, but much of this was swept away when the tide of commerce demanded more and larger warehouses. Those in existence now, some of them of vast proportions, date from the 1860's — some of the more recent examples date from the 1880's and 1890's. Few were built after the turn of the century.

As we walk along Chaloner Street, a glance to the right reveals the aforementioned bowstring girder swing bridge spanning the passage between Wapping and Queen's Docks and, nearer at hand, at the south end of the Wapping Warehouse stand two further examples of Jesse Hartley's ancient stone towers. One of them, the tallest, once contained hydraulic machinery, the smaller, conical tower being a "sentry post" used by dock watchmen or police. The hydraulic tower bears the date 1855.

Between Norfolk Street and Brick Street along the east side of the dock road stands a rather ornate building — the Chaloner Street goods depot of the Great Western Railway, which as mentioned earlier, has no rail access of its own into Liverpool. Even the docks railway passes their depot by with no connection, leaving road motors to deal with the traffic.

A lengthy single-storey ancient transit shed on the right-hand side of Chaloner Street hides Queen's Dock from view and presently the intersection of Parliament Street and the dock road is reached, with the large African Oil Mills on the north corner. Here the dock road changes its name yet again — to Sefton Street (after the Earl of Sefton). Proceeding onwards Stanhope Street is shortly reached, and opposite its junction with the dock road lies the watery expanse of Coburg Dock. Situated transversely to the river, this originated as the Union Dock in 1816, and had an outer basin which subsequently vanished when the two were made into one in 1858, the large dock thus produced being named Coburg. A bowstring girder swing bridge crosses the passage between Queen's and Coburg Docks.

The most prominent objects in the vicinity now are two immense grain silos, one old and one new, which loom mightily above Sefton Street on the riverward side. The old one, in red brickwork, was opened in 1906 and at that time was the worlds largest granary. It is owned by the Liverpool Grain Storage & Transit Company. The newer silo was built in 1936, and is in striking contrast to its neighbour, being an enormous concrete "block" with a smaller one on the top. Several ventilators on the roof are of curious shape and at a distance look like a group of large birds! A covered bridge of recent construction links the two buildings at considerable height above the street. Floating grain elevators in the adjacent dock transfer grain from ships into the capacious bins of the silos.

Railway lines laid in concrete with some quite complicated trackwork front the concrete silo, whilst a single line laid in granite setts passes through the older building via a lengthy colonade on the dock side. A single-line branch diverges from the main line here, which becomes two long sidings running westwards between the transit sheds of Queen's No. 1 Branch and Coburg Docks. This branch was laid in 1923.

Immediately on the south side of Coburg Dock, on the river frontage there is a small harbour-like area known as the South Ferry Basin. Back in the last century a steamer plied to and from Tranmere, berthing in this tiny haven. Here too, are several small docks used by fishing craft, small coasters and yachts. One bay is used by the MD & HB as a store for marker buoys and light-ships. Here grass grows on the quays, yet only a little distance away large ships are moored and all is hustle and business. This quaint little backwater still retains an aura of the past, just like Canning Dock near the city centre which we passed earlier-on. There is however, one small hive of activity — a ship repair works with a foundry etc., and railway track in quite an elaborate pattern, completely separate from the docks railway serves the premises. It is used by steam travelling cranes which convey materials between the works and quayside. One of these lines ends at right-angles to the edge of the quay — with no buffers!

Passing the junction of Sefton Street and the appropriately-titled Hill Street, part of which was once traversed by horse-drawn trams, we note on our right, the Brunswick Dock station of the Overhead Railway, which is in the shadow of the previously-mentioned concrete grain silo which rears above to a great height. Passengers coming down the stairs from the platforms must keep a careful look-out for their safety because of the large amount of motor and rail traffic on the roadway at this busy location.

The next item of railway interest lies at the north corner of Warwick Street where it joins Sefton Street. This is the remains of the bombed ex-L&NW goods station, a rather small establishment with two separate single-line branches leading across the road from the docks railway to serve it. Both branches are laid in bull-head rail with a wide check-rail and paved with stone setts. This goods station was opened in 1897. On the opposite side of Warwick Street there is a much more extensive war ruin, the large South Docks goods station of the former Lancashire & Yorkshire Railway, built in 1882. This installation was burned out completely together with a great many railway wagons, and smouldered for weeks. It was a scene of utter devastation in December 1940 and appeared to be a stupendous task to clear, but this was eventually done. Now its wagon turntables and rails lie buried beneath the rubble and debris, over which grass and weeds have spread a colourful dress. The yard, all that was left, was beyond use for merchandise after the bombing, but occasionally wagons were shunted into it in order to relieve the sidings on the dock estate. A double line connection with the dockside railway crosses Sefton Street at the North end of the goods station. At the rear, on higher ground runs Caryl Street (formerly Harrington Street) with its 1930's vintage tenements. Separated from the South Docks goods station by a brick wall is yet another, built by the L&NWR, and this too was heavily bombed though not rendered useless. The stone-setted yard contains four sidings in two groups. Some distance apart from each other, each with a connection to the docks main line across Sefton Street.

Not so far beyond the aforementioned goods station, Northumberland Street joins Sefton Street, and on the south side of Northumberland Street stands an immense building in clean red brickwork, and of quite handsome design. This is the Brunswick Dock goods station of the Cheshire Lines Railway. This structure, which was built about the turn of the century is fireproof, and it somehow escaped serious damage in the blitz, even though it presented the largest railway target in the area. The pleasant little building that looks like a house, standing near the south corner of Northumberland Street, was the office of the original Cheshire Lines Brunswick Station, at which all trains terminated until Liverpool Central station was opened in 1874. At the rear of the large depot is a much older one, still in use, erected when the railway first came in 1864. The land slopes quite steeply upwards from the dock road and an area had to be cut out of the sandstone to accommodate the goods depot and sidings etc.

The lengthy, wide dock after which the railway stations in this area are named, was opened in 1832. It was the first dock built by Jesse Hartley and was intended mainly for use by the timber trade. Originally there were two large graving docks at the south end and these covered the site of the old Tide Mill reservoirs that were known as "Jackson's Dam". Later extensions obliterated the graving docks along with Queen Anne Street South, which parallelled Sefton Street on the riverward side between Stanhope Street and Hill Street.

On the west side of Sefton Street, behind the dock wall is the Mersey Docks & Harbour Board's Brunswick locomotive shed, a new one built in 1945 to replace an older one which was destroyed during the wartime air-raids. Here also, a branch from the docks main line curves to cross the swing bridge over the passage between

Brunswick and Toxteth Docks, the last-named being entirely circumnavigated by railway lines, whilst there are several lengthy sidings on the east side of the dock. The southern extremity of the Cheshire Lines goods station is at Park Street (named after Toxteth Park) which joins Sefton Street here and almost opposite is Toxteth Dock station of the Overhead Railway. Park Street rises steeply, passing above several lines that lead into Brunswick goods station, which are bounded on their east side by Caryl Street. The CLC main line into Liverpool curves inland here, and enters a lengthy tunnel. An extensive railway yard with many sidings occupies the east side of Sefton Street, and from this yard there emerge two spur lines, widely separated, which give connections between the Cheshire Lines and Mersey Docks & Harbour Board Railways. This is a very busy place for both rail and road traffic, with always something moving.

The next dock reached is Toxteth, which was opened in 1888. At its southern extremity Toxteth joins Harrington Dock by a passage which is spanned by a swing bridge with railway tracks upon it. Harrington Dock swallowed up the site of the small Egerton Dock which was situated a little way north of the foot of Egerton Street (later renamed Harlow Street). The Harrington Dock was built by the Harrington Dock Company, but did not last for very long under private management, for it was sold to the Dock Trustees, forerunners of the Mersey Docks & Harbour Board, in 1843, and later enlarged.

In like manner to Toxteth Dock, Harrington is completely surrounded by railway tracks. Opposite the foot of Wellington Road is the Herculaneum Dock station of the Overhead Railway and a massive iron footbridge leads from this station to Grafton Street, crossing the dock road and a number of railway tracks including the CLC Liverpool-Manchester main line, also the busy Brunswick locomotive shed of the Cheshire Lines system. Grafton Street is at a much higher level than the dock road and here the Overhead Railway turns inland, crossing the road and rail yards on a lengthy lattice girder bridge, to plunge directly into a tunnel, the portal of which is high up in the rock face. Here it becomes an underground railway as far as its terminus at Park Road in the district known as Dingle.

At the foot of Beresford Road, the old South End ferry stage once occupied the piece of shore that is now covered by Harrington Dock. From this stage two small passenger steamers sailed to and from New Ferry on the Cheshire side of the Mersey many years ago.

The very last group of docks in the long line that stretches all the way from Seaforth is Herculaneum, which consists of a "wet" dock and three graving docks, these dry docks for ship repairs being parallel with the river. The dock, occupying the foreshore once known as "Pottery Beach", was opened in 1864 but has since been modified and extended. It was of course, called after the famous Herculaneum Pottery which existed here between about 1794 and 1841 and known far and wide for its fine ware, specimens of which can be seen in the city Museum. At Herculaneum Dock, Sefton Street, the long dock road, comes to its southern terminal at a dockyard gateway, without making connection to any other major thoroughfare here.

Herculaneum Dock is used almost exclusively for bunkering ships with fuel oil or coal. There are several hydraulic coaling cranes which lift railway wagons bodily and tilt them so that the coal falls directly into the ships bunkers. The coal comes in trainloads via the Cheshire Lines Railway, and so also, does some of the oil fuel.

The docks railway, with numerous sidings continues along the east side of Herculaneum Dock, then, having reached the south end, curves westwards and after running past part of the wet dock and the graving docks, turns again to run parallel with the river to the southern extremity of Dingle Oil Yards, bounded by large numbers of oil storage tanks on the east side and mud banks on the river side. There is a small MD&HB locomotive shed at the south end of No. 2 graving dock, in which is housed a fireless locomotive that works in the vicinity of the oil installations, ordinary steam locomotives being banned from the area. There was another fireless locomotive here also, until 1940, in which year it was destroyed, being inside Brunswick locomotive shed which received a direct hit by a bomb during an air-raid.

Two long jetties project into the Mersey in this locality, one near Herculaneum Dock (North Dingle Jetty) and the other from Dingle Point (South Dingle Jetty). Beyond this southern extremity of the docks lies a stretch of muddy beach known to generations of Liverpolitans as the "Cast Iron Shore" — "Cassie" to the children, a semi-derelict area opposite the Devil's Sandbank in the river. The Dingle oil jetties were built in 1922 to enable oil tankers to unload without the necessity of coming inside the docks.

When the oil tank farm was built, in 1921, it occupied land on which formerly stood "Dingle Bank", the old home of the Cropper family. It existed from the 1820's until demolition in 1919.

We have now reached the end of the long trek, on foot, along the dock road, noting chiefly the railway installations with little reference to ships, but these can be seen to great advantage from the trains of the Liverpool Overhead Railway. To explore the interior of the dock estate on foot would require several weeks and would prove to be an arduous task. In the next chapter we will look at some of the changes that have affected the railway system of the docks, and the decline of the once great port, a rather sad record. A walk along the dock road in 1992 is an unpleasant experience for anyone who knew the docks in their heyday. Sic Transit Gloria indeed!

Coal for Ireland being tipped into ships hold. Bramley-Moore Dock. May 1960.
Photo — T. Taylor

A rail enthusiasts special train leaving Riverside station on Saturday, 20th April 1968. Class 5 4-6-0 locomotive No. 45305 which survives today in preservation.
Photo — J. Corkill

Riverside station, with a rail enthusiasts special train on Saturday, 13th June, 1964. A change from the Trans-Atlantic passengers of former years.
Photo — J. Corkill

Ancient trackwork at Nelson Dock still surviving in 1960. Locomotive No. 31 is in the background.   *Photo – T. Taylor*

Ancient rails at Albert Dock in 1960. These were later removed. Believed to have been last used about 1951.   Photo — T. Taylor

Fireless steam locomotive No. 1 of the C.E.G.B. shunts coal hoppers at Clarence Dock Power Station, May, 1960. Photo — T. Taylor

Avonside 0-6-0 Saddle Tank No. 16 at Brunswick Engine shed, May 1960. Photo — T. Taylor

CHAPTER THREE
The Receding Tide

The end of the war in 1945 gave little hint of things to come in the docks of Liverpool and Bootle. Enormous volumes of cargo continued to be handled, and passenger ships, re-converted from troop carriers, returned to their old routes and generally there was an air of confidence. Blitzed transit sheds were rebuilt, and river entrance locks were reconstructed at Waterloo, Langton and Canada Docks in the north and Brunswick Dock at the south end of the estate. Modernisation of other dock installations and cargo handling appliances was carried out and the future looked bright. Things were soon to change however and decline lay ahead due to several causes. There had of course been slumps in business on several occasions in the past, and that of the 1930's was still fresh in the memory, but things recovered and the docks survived. This time however, the decline for most of the docks was terminal.

Some of the reasons for the decline were the increased use of containers for cargo, the rise to spectacular new heights in business at several east coast ports, more convenient for a lot of shipping that formerly used Merseyside docks, fewer coasting vessels and tramp cargo ships. Modern traffic and economics saw increasing use of vastly larger ships which needed larger docks and thus could not be handled at most of the older Merseyside docks, particularly those at the south end. Once, when new docks were built no old ones were closed, but with construction of the Royal Seaforth Dock north of Gladstone group, many closures took place and a number of berths were mothballed.

The Royal Seaforth Dock, opened in 1973, has a water area of 85 acres and ten berths, each devoted to a particular traffic including timber, grain, containers and general merchandise. It also has roll-on, roll-off facilities and new road communications. At first, no rail facilities were provided, a fact that greatly surprised members of the Netherlands Chamber of Commerce when they paid a visit. It surprised many people in Liverpool too!

The Royal Seaforth Dock container/cargo area covered Muspratt's Estate on which were the timber yards and the MD & HB Engineering Department yard with its dozens of railway sidings. Part of the estate was latterly occupied by a scrap metal merchant — J. Routledge, who dismantled some BR steam locomotives and rolling stock during the great purge of the early 1960's, which saw vast reductions in rail lines, locomotives and rolling stock.

A colossal grain silo, powerful new cranes, an extensive container terminal and new road system have replaced the old Seaforth Sands of pleasant memory, and a visitor arriving on the scene after a few years of absence would scarcely recognise the place. Linked with the new Royal Seaforth Dock project has been the complete closure of the south docks — every single one of them from Canning to Herculaneum, which resulted in many of the premises along Strand Street, Wapping, Chaloner Street and Sefton Street becoming empty and derelict. Large numbers of warehouses and other buildings have been demolished amid avalanches of falling brickwork as the crane — swung steel balls strike, whilst their strong timber joists, after a century or more of load-bearing service, have been either put to other uses or burned. Indeed, the fragrant aroma of burning timbers has scented the Liverpool air for several years as the face of the city has undergone alteration, and long familiar landmarks obliterated. Closure of the south docks naturally affected the adjacent hinterland, so quite a vast area became derelict or semi-derelict. It seems almost incredible that such an extensive ghost area could develop in a busy city, but this has indeed happened in Liverpool, although some of the buildings have since been taken on short-term leases by various concerns. Even the extensive oil jetties and storage grounds at Dingle were shut down and subsequently swept away.

The most prominent alteration along the full length of the dock road was the closure of the Liverpool Overhead Railway, which took place on the wintry Sunday night of 30th December 1956. A long fight to save this much-loved railway was unsuccessful, and those last trains, one in each direction, were travelled on and watched by numerous people who turned out in the chill night air to pay their respects to their departing iron servant. The structure was demolished during 1957 and no longer could the dock road pedestrian keep out of the rain by walking beneath the "Docker's Umbrella". Its demise gave a strange bare look to the dock road along which it had cast a shadow for 63 years.

Now that tourism has become a major industry on Merseyside, many people say that the Overhead Railway, if it had servived, would be a valuable attraction. However, the reasons for the existence of the line have largely gone, namely the formerly busy docks with 17,000 dockers, not to mention the host of other dock area workers and the ceaseless streams of travellers between docks or ships and city. What would the visitor see from the railway today? Empty docks and empty land where busy industries and warehouses once stood, and an almost deserted dock road would not prove very attractive, and what would the situation be in the winter when the tourists had gone? Once fears that colossal losses would have forced closure sooner or later.

In the case of the freight-carrying railways, the events of 30 or so years have been extremely depressing, with closure after closure of lines and stations that served the dockland districts. Even the new Royal Seaforth Dock has only one single-track rail connection and all other lines in its vicinity have been swept away to accommodate the complex road system which serves the dock and its adjacent container base. North Mersey yard continued to deal with rail traffic for some time after its main-line connection was severed, trains thereafter being routed via Alexandra Dock and the ex-L & NW, Edge Hill-Bootle Branch. When the North Mersey Branch was in full use, trains to and from the docks were worked throughout by main-line locomotives, but these could not work over the dock lines between Alexandra Dock and North Mersey owing to the sharply-curved connections between the main-line system and the docks railway. However, one of the sharp curves was re-laid to main-line standards and the east-side dock line upgraded as a reserved track with heavy flat-bottom rails. This was carried out in 1970, and upon completion allowed the largest locomotives to run through to North Mersey and Gladstone Dock. The re-laid curve crosses Regent Road at Alexandra Dock station and is protected by standard level crossing flashing lights when a train crosses the road. The crossing saw little use over the following ten years until new developments brought regular traffic, of which more later.

The Langton Dock, ex-Midland Railway goods station, saw declining traffic in post-war years, and eventually weeds and brambles grew over disused rails as it was phased out. Before rail traffic ceased, in the late 1960's, part of the yard was given over to other than railway use, and it became a store for Lykes Lines, the American company, whose ships could be seen in the adjacent docks. Inevitably, containers were stacked in the yard and motor vehicles stood where railway wagons once were loaded or unloaded. The site, now completely cleared, belongs to the Merseyside Development Corporation.

In 1965 the extensive Alexandra Granaries in Lyster and Arctic Roads were demolished, and the space created soon became filled with motor vehicles and containers. The big boxes are to be seen everywhere along the north docks nowadays and it is interesting to note the various titles and colour schemes of their owning companies and to speculate upon the far-flung places to which they have travelled — by train, lorry and ship.

Alexandra Dock ex-L & NW goods station is still open (1988) but sees sparse traffic. The facilities have been considerably reduced and about half the premises have been given over to non-rail use. Only the central section sees any rail traffic nowadays, the yards at the north and south ends being used by industrial concerns. Actually, all the rails have been removed from the south-end yard but the smaller yard on the north side of Church Street still has most of its rails, buried under gravel and cement, and isolated by removal of the connection across Church Street. Condemned goods wagons seemed to be the main occupants of the main yard during 1986-1988, enroute to a metal shearing plant at Seaforth.

The other ex-L & NWR goods station at Canada Dock saw gradually declining use until 1983, in which year it was closed completely and all the rails removed. Indeed, some sections of the extensive yard had ceased to handle rail traffic by the early 1960's. Canada Dock depot was formerly a busy interchange point between the LMS lines and the docks railway. The rails crossing Regent Road still existed in 1988, leading to a vast, derelict empty site, only the post-war transit shed still standing.

The blitzed Great Central Railway goods depot at Lower Bank View became an engineer's depot for the Mersey Docks & Harbour Board, and a new building occupies the site. Although the rails in the yard have long gone, the connection across Regent Road still remained in 1987, the track ending abruptly at the gateway.

The ex-Lancashire & Yorkshire Railway goods depot known as Bankfield & Canada has been completely closed and all track removed. In 1988 the site was occupied by a new grain silo, having been put to various temporary uses since closure in the mid-1960's. The 1960's saw also the closure of other former L & Y Railway establishments — the large and extensive North Docks goods station which lay between Regent Road and Great Howard Street, together with the coal branch to Bramley-Moore Dock. The site of North Docks station inevitably became a road transport base. It is difficult to recognise these former railway strongholds nowadays, but rails leading from the dockside line ending at blank walls or in overgrown rubble-strewn ground provide clues. The tarmacing of some roads has covered rails which will be discovered in years to come when road repair work will reveal them!

The group of sidings alongside the United Molasses depot on Sandhills Lane were left in position for several years after they ceased to be regularly used in the mid-1960's, but have now gone, the Molasses depot having been extended over the site, with further storage tanks and buildings. The single line connection over Regent Road still remained in place in late 1987, ending abruptly at the former gates of the railway yard. Tank lorries now stand on the site of the sidings.

The old established and extensive goods station of the former London & North Western Railway at Waterloo Dock was closed in 1963, except for a siding which served the adjacent seed mills, which was retained for a couple of years longer. A ventilating tower for the Wallasey road tunnel was built in the former railway yard alongside Waterloo Road, but the rails that connected the depot with the MD & HB line were left in position with the peculiar result that they ended suddenly at the gate of the ventilating plant! Another part of the goods station area, alongside Oil Street became a gypsy encampment, so the site certainly changed its role drastically, and no doubt will do so again with redevelopment of the district. It was empty and derelict in 1988.

Closure of Riverside station, reached via Waterloo Dock, has already been mentioned, but the single line across Waterloo Road was still in situ in 1988 isolated from the main line at Edge Hill by $1\frac{1}{2}$ miles of empty tunnel!

In 1970 the combined lifting and swing bridge over Stanley Dock passage was demolished, the adjacent road bridge remaining. This action cut the docks railway at this point so that the lines only extended from Nelson Dock to Gladstone, all docks between the former and Princes thus having no rail access. A new terminal for the Irish shipping services was developed at Waterloo and Trafalgar Docks and brought into full use in October 1972, but it has no rail connection, most of the tracks having been removed or put out of use. Even a long section of the docks main line has been asphalted over at Victoria Dock to make a smooth road for cars, and lorries carrying containers.

In 1971-2 the huge Sandon Dock warehouse of the former Midland Railway was demolished, its absence creating a very noticeable gap in the skyline. The associated railway yards were closed in April 1968. A semaphore signal, at "danger" guarded the entrance from the docks railway for many weeks after all the rail had been removed from this once-busy yard! Lonely among the weeds, it seemed to symbolise the retreat of the railways from Liverpool's dockland where they had once been of enormous importance.

Stanley Tobacco Warehouse lost its rail connection soon after the Second World War and no trace of track remains. The North Stanley Dock Warehouse likewise had its long branch line removed, but a short length of track still remained at the gates in 1973, the cross-road connection with the docks railway having been lifted. Rails and turntables still exist in the warehouse in 1991, however.

The docks "main line" between Princes Dock and Wapping had been largely disused since about September 1961, when trips between Park Lane goods depot and Huskisson were abandoned, so that only an occasional train traversed the section across the Pier Head area after that date. Even so, such trains had to run during the night and complete their trips before 6.30 am, because by day hundreds of motorists parked their cars on the rails! Actually months went by between trains and even then, only the southbound track was used, the northbound track having been disused on the latter section since 1964. After 1965 or so, the only trains that normally worked north of King's Dock were those for the Guinness transit shed on the east side of Salthouse Dock, but even this traffic ceased in 1970. The very last train to traverse the Pier Head section is believed to have run on Sunday, 7th February 1971 — many months after a previous train, so that the wheel flanges churned a great deal of grit and rubbish from the rusty rails. After this date the track became unusable owing to road and drainage works which resulted in concrete being spread across in places, whilst a building was erected on the track near Georges Dock gates. New road works at Pier Head undertaken in the early 1980's have covered the land formerly occupied by the railway.

The ex-L & Y goods depots at Wapping saw reduced rail traffic after the war, resulting in sale of the 1914 shed on the north side of Ansdell Street to a motor firm, the rails inside soon being concreted over. The branch from the docks line leading to it remained in the roadway for many years however, but in 1961 the points connecting it to the main line were removed. The older depot, on the south side of Ansdell Street remained in use until June 1959, when it too was closed, and afterwards lay empty and derelict until demolition in 1967. The points of the 'Y' connection to the docks main line from this depot were removed in October 1965. The empty site of the old depot was, somewhat inevitably, turned into a car park. The Merseyside Police HQ and car park, built in the early 1980's, completely cover the site of the two goods depots now, whilst Ansdell Street and Salthouse Lane have vanished.

The great goods station at Park Lane was closed in October 1965 and gradually demolished, only the massive walls being left. As late as 1976 the branch from the docks railway still remained in the roadway, to end at the gates of what had become an empty wasteland. Demolition of the extensive warehouses rendered the tunnel portals visible from the dock road, and on viewing the site today it is hard to imagine the hive of railway activity which the depot was in its heyday. In the summer of 1976 the site became an industrial estate, with a new road running right up to the tunnel portals.

The former L & NW depot at Warwick Street, destroyed in the war, was replaced by a new building, but not by the railway authorities. The site was sold and became a depot of SPD Ltd., but the original rail connections with the docks railway were retained and rail traffic resumed for a few years, but road transport had taken over completely by the mid-1960's. The two lines crossing Sefton Street remained in position until 1982.

Chaloner Street goods depot of the former Great Western Railway was closed on 1st December 1956, and later sold to a road transport concern. It was still a lorry depot in 1974. It will be remembered that this depot had no rail connections with the docks railway, being served entirely by road motors. By the summer of 1976 the building had become empty and derelict, but after a period of use by Guinness Exports Ltd., was empty again in 1988.

The ex-L & Y South Docks goods station which was completely destroyed during the air-raids of 1940 lay derelict for many years after the war, the rails and turntables having been removed and the rubble largely cleared. What remained became overgrown with grass, and a great variety of colourful weeds made the site quite picturesque. The tranquil peace was disturbed during 1964 however, when the builders moved in and constructed a road transport depot on the site. This has now gone and in 1988 the empty site was earmarked for housing. The former L & NWR goods station "next door" at the south end was used by British Road Services for a time after the war, and later by a private haulage contractor. The rails were left in position for many years in the stone-setted yard. By 1988 the depot had vanished.

Brunswick, the ex-Cheshire Lines Railway goods station outlived all others on the south docks until April 1971, when all rail traffic ceased. It had become a dead-end by then however, for rail traffic on the south docks estate had ceased in March 1970. The great warehouse building still proclaiming GREAT NORTHERN, MANCHESTER, SHEFFIELD & LINCOLNSHIRE & MIDLAND RAILWAYS in letters of stone stood derelict until 1974 when demolition took place. It was the end also of the old passenger station building that had been used as an office since the line was extended to Central Station, Liverpool in 1872. Complete closure of the south docks was the chief reason for the closure of Brunswick. The only trains passing the site today are Merseyrail electric trains on the Southport-Hunts Cross service. No goods sidings remain.

An enormous amount of controversy raged over the future of the south docks — particularly have passions been aroused over the Albert Dock, that monument to Jesse Hartley, which, with its vast, deserted warehouses looming above now-quiet waters, awaited a fate that may not have been pleasant. Closure of the docks could not, of course, mean that they should lay derelict for evermore in a vast industrial wasteland. Many different ideas for their future use were put forward by interested bodies and organisations, but nothing definite was done until the formation, in 1981, of the Merseyside Development Corporation. At last, positive plans for the south docks area were drawn up and new schemes put in hand to revitalise the area which had become almost a dreadful no-man's-land of decay and dereliction. Since 1981 a drastic change has come to the once busy dock road between the Pier Head and Herculaneum, the wrecking cranes and bulldozers having been used with great vigour among the old property.

From the Pier Head, as far as Parliament Street, the dock road (The Strand and Wapping) has been turned into a dual carriageway and almost all the old buildings on its east side have been demolished, thus destroying the old "Sailor Town" image, except that one building from the sailing ship days, the "Baltic Fleet" public house, has escaped the bulldozers. Most of the vast warehouses in the side streets have also gone. Today the vast Police Headquarters building occupies a fair length of the road, otherwise empty sites have been landscaped.

Beyond Parliament Street the east side of the dock road (Sefton Street) has not altered greatly so far, many of the old buildings being again occupied on short-term leases. Land released by warehouse demolition has in many cases been claimed for light industrial use, with streets that once seemed like canyons now having only small buildings in place of the former fortress-like warehouses.

The west side of the dock road from the Pier Head to Herculaneum has been drastically altered. The section as far as the Wapping warehouses has been turned into a promenade, paved with granite setts, provided with new lighting in "period style", and trees planted at intervals. The old dockside sheds with their crazy-paving walls have gone, only the south-end arched wall of the East Salthouse shed having been retained as an historic artifact. A short length of rail was left in position here for a time, but was subsequently removed. The docks "main line" has completely vanished between Princes Dock gates and Herculaneum except for the siding and loop on Canning Dock north quay, which hopefully will be preserved. Re-surfacing of the dock road has meant the disappearance of all the railway crossings, but in spite of vast new works some track still survived within the dock walls in 1988.

In connection with the International Garden Festival held in 1984, Herculaneum Dock was filled-in with 750,000 tons of sand, to become a car park for the festival, whilst Brunswick railway yard was also used for parking purposes. It was up for sale in 1988. Harrington and Toxteth of the longitudinal docks have been filled-in, as have most of the transverse docks, but the remainder of the longitudinal docks have been retained, minus their transit sheds, and a water course remains throughout from Brunswick to Canning. Swing bridges have been replaced by fixed bridges.

The two enormous grain silos at Coburg Dock were still in use in 1988, but were served entirely by road transport. Much of the former rail track was still in place here in mid-1988. This complex is the last of the south docks installations to remain in use for its original purpose.

The extensive oil depots and tank farm at Dingle were swept away to make land available for the Festival Gardens, whilst many new houses have been built on former industrial sites in the area. Grafton Street gas works remains as a holder station. Much new housing, in old dockside streets, has greatly altered the character of the district.

Virtually the only dock complex to retain its old character is the Albert, the enormous warehouses, after an uneasy sleep under constant threat for many years, at last were saved to the great relief of historians and industrial archaeologists. The Albert Dock Company Limited was formed to re-develop the site into "Albert Dock Village", a complex of shops and offices, conference and exhibition centre, art gallery, sports centre and residential apartments.The north block of Albert warehouse became part of the Merseyside Maritime Museum, whilst the former hydraulic pumping station of 1875, with its beautiful chimney has become a pub-restaurant. The remaining blocks of warehouses have become shops, restaurants, an art gallery and apartments. The dock itself remains, as does Canning and Salthouse, whilst a small portion of the former Dukes Dock has been retained.

Various interested bodies on Merseyside had been pressing for projects such as these for years, often with a feeling that all might be lost. There was even a suggestion that a transport museum might be formed with steam trains operating on the old quays, but the original rails alongside the North Albert warehouse were dug out for scrap in 1972, leaving only a short stretch of the single approach line on the east side of the swing bridge, the latter being a modern one that replaced the original bridge in 1961, but saw little use as the dock ceased to be used soon afterwards. The new bridge was not provided with rails, so that rail access to Albert Dock was severed. The points at which the Albert branch joined the docks "main line" were removed in October 1960, and most regrettably the rails leading to the dock road were removed in 1984 when the area was re-paved to form the entrance to the "Albert Dock Village". A short length of new track, using modern components has been laid alongside the north warehouse block on the site of the former rails but is unlikely to be used to run "museum" trains as it is too short. A rail-built stop-block has been placed at each end of this new track, each being fitted with buffers from scrapped goods wagons in non-railwaylike manner, as sidings did not usually have the refinement of spring buffers!

Directly opposite Albert Dock, the site of the former great domed Custom House is completely changed, being now occupied by the ultra-modern "Steers House" with its huge glass expanses reflecting the light. This building is named after Thomas Steers, the engineer who built the "Old Dock" in the pool in 1715. "Steers House" stands where sailing ships once tied up, until the dock was filled-in during the 1820's and the Custom House built on the site. As noted earlier, this edifice was destroyed by bombs in 1940.

Steers and Hartley have been largely forgotten for ages, their names only emerging into the limelight in very recent times with the sudden interest in industrial archaeology engendered by the destruction on an enormous scale of former industrial buildings and installations. We still await a suitable memorial to Hartley, especially as so much of his handywork is being swept away, though his greatest achievement, the Albert Dock, commemorates him. Perhaps a "Hartley House" or "Hartley Place" would be fitting, because the dock buildingss will always be referred to as the "Albert".

Reverting to earlier events in the run-down of the docks in the post-war era, we are faced with a sad list of banishments. The ancient and immensely interesting Duke's Warehouse of 1811 was demolished during 1965, its place being taken by a new single-storey transit shed serving King's Dock, but this had a short life, becoming redundant when the south docks were closed. It was subsequently dismantled and re-erected elsewhere.

Not long after the closure of the rail system on the south docks had taken place, the possible demise of the remainder of the system was hinted at by the Mersey Docks & Harbour Company (the body that replaced the Mersey Docks & Harbour Board). Figures were produced to support a case for closure, which revealed that the railway, on the north docks estate, was vastly under-used. It was stated that during World War II, in one year alone (1944), the railway handled 4,145,408 tons of merchandise. By 1972 the figure had fallen to a mere 150,000 tons. Truly the motor-truck had assumed almost a monopoly of the docks traffic, but as events turned out there would be little docks traffic even for road transport a few years hence, apart from that at the Royal Seaforth Dock.

The threatened closure of the railway became a reality in 1973, the final train being run on Tuesday, 11th September of that year. A diesel locomotive of the MD & H Company hauled the few wagons that were on the dock estate from the south-west quay of Alexandra Dock to the British Rail yard at Alexandra, thus ending yet one more era of transport on Merseyside. This seemed to be the end, but six years later trains made a come-back! A rail link to the Royal Seaforth Dock was eventually made, using a length of the still intact dockside railway, from Alexandra Dock BR depot to Seaforth Sands, one track only (east side) being re-laid to main-line standards, on its own reservations and could be used by the largest main-line locomotives. Container trains on regular schedules commenced to use this line on 11th February 1980.

The Royal Seaforth Dock container terminal occupies land that was formerly the Muspratt estate and before the new dock was made, the MD & HB Engineer's yard and Lamb Bro's timber yards. The rail line has been extended almost to the most northerly extent of the dock complex at Waterloo. Here too, was established a metal shearing plant which dealt with scrap of all kinds, including railway wagons and during 1986-87 long trains of condemned steel mineral and hopper wagons, together with many goods brake vans were worked from Edge Hill to Alexandra Dock depot, where they were left to await their end.

In August 1985, the MD & HB line from the dock road into Hornby Dock was revived and used for the export of scrap metal which came in train-loads via the Edge Hill-Bootle branch. British Rail locomotives hauled the trains into the dock area, where only MD & HB engines formerly ventured but nowadays no locomotives are owned by the Dock Company. A BR Class 08 diesel-electric locomotive was hired to do the work in 1987, however. Some export traffic in railway equipment went via Hornby Dock in 1987-88.

Apart from the closure of most of the dockside railway, decline in shipping using the port has meant that many quays and docks or parts of docks have been closed or mothballed. In 1988 the following docks (or berths) remained in partial or full use mainly for bulk cargoes: Gladstone, Hornby, Alexandra, West Langton, Brocklebank, Canada, Huskisson, Sandon, Wellington, Bramley-Moore, Nelson, Salisbury, Collingwood, Clarence, Waterloo East and Princes Half-Tide East. Only Hornby and Gladstone are rail-connected. Brocklebank Dock is also used for freight and passenger services to and from Ireland.

Along the dock road many of the former industries have closed, especially those concerned with shipping and ship repairs, their buildings, in some instances, being used by different concerns, whilst many new buildings have been erected after bomb damage or demolition. The once teeming highway is much quieter nowadays.

As so much of the docks railway has been removed, built over or buried, reinstatement would be an expensive and difficult task even if the tide turned in favour of rail transit again. For the time being then, fleets of lorries and a few trains move the containers to and from the 50,000 tonne ships at Royal Seaforth, whilst lorries serve the smaller vessels at the rest of the docks. Perhaps the Channel Tunnel will bring Liverpool more business, but even if it does, the operations will be vastly different from those of even very recent times.

A walk along the dock road nowadays seems deadly quiet to a person who saw it in past years, and only in the mind's eye can one see the gas lamps, oil lamps, water columns, stone setts and cobbles, sailors, dock workers, transport men, the "judies", men of all nations and those bands of coolies who walked in single file. Also hundreds of horses, steam wagons, motor lorries, locomotives, and in earlier times, the horse-drawn omnibuses running on the dock railway, the tea rooms, cocoa rooms and dockside pubs — most, if not all, now vanished into history.

MD&HB 0-6-0 Saddle Tank No. 1, the oldest engine in the fleet, now preserved in the Liverpool Museum. It is seen here at Huskisson in November, 1960. Note the fire-irons.   Photo — J.F. Ward

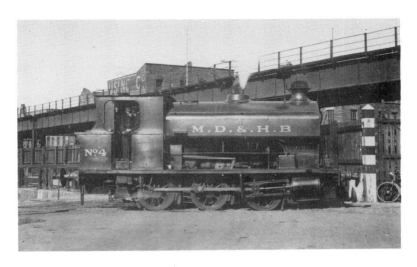

*MD&HB Large Avonside 0-6-0 Saddle Tank No. 4 near Canada Dock,
September 1950.* Photo — K.J. Cooper collection

*MD&HB Avonside 0-6-0 Saddle Tank No. 24 beneath the bridgework of the
Liverpool Overhead Railway in June, 1957.* Photo — F. Jones

Avonside 0-6-0 Saddle Tank with steam to spare, near North Mersey.
September 1963. Photo — F. Dean

MD&HB 0-6-0 Barclay Fireless locomotive at Brunswick Dock. July 1935.
Photo — J.A. Peden collection

MD&HB Hunslet 0-6-0 Saddle Tank No. 31 at Canada Dock, August, 1958, travelling beneath the Overhead Railway.   Photo — J.A. Peden

A train of meat containers trundles along beneath the "Docker's Umbrella" behind Hunslet 0-6-0 Saddle Tank No. 8. Circa 1958. Photo — J.A. Peden

CHAPTER FOUR

Iron Horses of the Dock Road

The "Dock Line of Railway" as the system was officially known was originally intended to facilitate construction of docks and associated works, and was worked by horses for no less than 60 years or so due to the fear of sparks from steam locomotives setting buildings and cargoes alight. Nevertheless, a steam locomotive was occasionally seen on the dock road, usually owned by contractors or traders.

In May 1865, the contractor T. Monk was granted permission to use a locomotive for hauling debris from excavations east of Sefton Street to Harrington Dock, thence to be hauled northwards by horses. No other locomotive appeared until 1874 when the contractor C. Tottenham was given permission to use a steam engine in connection with new north docks works and a location on the east side of Regent Road. C. Tottenham was the contractor on the Alexandra Dock construction, and used fourteen locomotives on the task, but the engine used on the dock road was required to be fitted with a spark-arrestor and was not to exceed four miles per hour, with a flagman walking ahead of it.

The far-flung London & North Western railway reached Canada Dock in 1866 and had to use horses for traffic over the dock lines, but in January 1875 that company received permission to use a light steam locomotive to haul timber between the north timber yard and the Canada Dock goods station. Again, the engine had to have a spark-arrestor and obey the four miles per hour speed limit and have a man with flags walking in front. The permission was granted only because the severe winter weather being experienced at the time made the work very difficult for the horses. In December of the same year they were allowed to use an engine between their station and land north of Battery Street.

Even the MD & HB Engineering Department had to apply to the Railway Committee for permission to use steam locomotives. In November 1875 the engineer obtained leave to use a small locomotive on the dock line, but only overnight between 8.00 pm and 8.00 am, and was not to exceed walking pace! A man carrying a red lamp had to precede the engine on foot, but on the light summer nights he carried a flag until darkness fell, and after daylight returned in the mornings.

In 1876 the Lancashire & Yorkshire Storage Company were allowed to use a small locomotive between Canada Half-Tide Dock and Canada goods station. The weight of the engine was not to exceed 12 tons, had to burn coke and be fitted with a spark-arrestor. The usual regulations regarding slow speed and flagman had to be observed.

Also in 1876, the contractor T. Monk was given permission to use a small locomotive between new works at the south gateway of Sandon Graving Dock and the north end, also for use of another small engine during the night only, between construction works at Herculaneum Dock and Waterloo Dock. Permission was only granted because there was difficulty in obtaining horses.

In March 1882 permission to use small locomotives on the dock line was granted as follows: The London & North Western Company between Canada goods station, the new Alexandra Dock goods station and Canada Street which was inside the dock estate; T. Monk between North Mersey and Bankfield; MD & HB Engineering Department between the south-east gate of Sandon Graving Dock and Strand Road. In every case the engines had to be equipped with a spark-arrestor, be accompanied by a flagman and not exceed a speed of three miles per hour.

In August 1883, the L & NWR sought permission to run a steam locomotive between Wapping goods station and Brunswick Dock, but permission was refused.

There were always strict rules, imposed by the Liverpool Health Committee, on the number of wagons forming a train on the dock road. The police kept watch and fines were imposed if any train exceeded the permitted length. The L & Y Company were fined five shillings in 1886. The bench considered that the bye-laws should be amended, and this was done, so that trains of 12 wagons could be run (hauled by horse teams) between the L & Y stations of North Mersey and Bankfield.

Owing to congestion, the slow pace of horse haulage (it needed five horses to haul a train of six wagons) and ever-increasing traffic, the Mersey Dock Authority began to look more favourably on the employment of steam locomotives, realising that things soon had to change. In March 1889, the L & Y Company were granted permission to use a light locomotive on timber traffic between Battery Street yard and Bankfield, subject to the usual regulations.

In October 1890, Messrs Eckersley, Godfrey and Liddelow were given permission to use a steam locomotive on the dock road. They were contractors engaged on new construction at Canada and

Hornby Docks. Use of the engine was subject to the slow-speed and flagman rule, and a spark-arrestor on the engine. Several other engines were employed by them within the dock works.

The Lancashire & Yorkshire Railway Company continually pressed for the introduction of locomotives for all traffic, and finally, in July 1894 were allowed to use an engine experimentally, subject to the usual regulations but in additon had to be fitted with a bell that tolled continuously as the engine travelled, and this rule persisted into the diesel age 50 years or so later!

On Monday, 13th May 1895, locomotives were at last permitted on the dock lines. No engine was to exceed a weight of $1\frac{1}{2}$ tons per foot on the track. The maximum train was to be 12 wagons and a minimum interval between trains was to be five minutes.

The Lancashire & Yorkshire Company set to work one of their 0-4-0 Saddle Tank "Pug" engines, No. 1288, burning oil-fuel in May 1895, and more followed. In 1897 the L & NWR equipped an 0-4-0 Saddle Tank engine, No. 3015, for burning oil and placed it in service along the dock road.

In October 1897, Edward Alcott, a timber merchant on Regent Road, was granted permission to use a locomotive on the MD & HB lines for hauling his traffic landed at the south docks. The engine was to burn oil and be fitted with a spark-arrestor and bell. By this time the Liverpool Overhead Railway had been opened and all engines working along the dock line, which ran directly beneath that railway, had to have a baffle plate above the chimney to divert smoke and steam away from the bridgeworks.

Alcott's first locomotive was "Pioneer", an 0-4-0 Saddle Tank built by Pecketts of Bristol in 1898. He obtained a second engine from the same makers in the same year, another 0-4-0 Saddle Tank named "Progress". The first was sold to the Vernon Petroleum Company at Penarth, whilst "Progress" was purchased by the shipping line T & J Harrison, who used it until 1907, when it was purchased by the Mersey Docks & Harbour Board and became their No. 5. It was sold in November 1915. Alcott's engine shed was under the west platform of Princes Dock "Overhead" station, but was moved to Hornby Dock in 1900.

In October 1902, the contractors for the granary at Coburg Dock were allowed to use a steam locomotive on the dock railway, whilst in 1905 the contractors Monk & Newell were given permission to use a locomotive for hauling materials between King's Dock and Hornby Dock, and to erect an engine shed at the latter. This shed was purchased by the MD & HB in 1911.

In November 1905, the speed limit for trains on the dock lines was raised from four to five miles per hour. In December 1906, trains could be formed of up to 14 wagons experimentally.

It was not until 1905 that the MD & HB commenced to work traffic with their own locomotives, using engines from the Engineering Department at first, but the purchase of additional engines was slow — the Board possessed only 16 by 1912.

In 1906 the Great Central Railway established a goods station on the north docks at Regent Road. A haulage contractor W. J. Lee was employed to haul GC traffic between this depot and Brunswick using an oil-burning locomotive. This engine was withdrawn in 1911 and Great Central engines took over the work.

In March 1911, train lengths could be increased to 18 wagons between 9.00 pm and 6.00 am. Speed could now be eight miles per hour, but no train was to exceed a length of 108 yards.

An odd occurence on 13th May 1907 was a collision between engine No. 4 and an electric tram at the crossing of the dock road and Water Street. No. 4 also disgraced itself by demolishing the doors of a transit shed on the dockside.

During the Great War of 1914-18 the Mersey docks had to deal with greatly-increased traffic, which meant the purchase of additonal locomotives and the provison of extra sidings. Fortunately there were no air-raids to contend with as was the case in the 1939-45 war. Tonnage hauled in 1914 was 450,000. In 1916 697,000 tons were hauled by the Board's engines.

Whenever heavy works or new dock construction was in progress, engines were borrowed from the MD & HB Traffic Department. When the new Gladstone North docks were being built during 1926-7, seven locomotives were transferred to the Engineers Department, but on return were proposed for sale as they probably needed heavy repairs. All were built between 1905 and 1913.

Space available is insufficient to include here details such as engine fleet and works numbers, construction dates etc. Sufficient to say that the type most favoured was the standard 0-6-0 outside-cylinder (14x20 ins) Saddle Tank, produced by the Avonside Engine Company of Bristol. A few engines by other manufacturers came and went, and so did some Avonside machines, but during the years 1937-1941 a number of inside-cylinder (15x20 ins) 0-6-0 Saddle Tank engines were obtained from the Hunslet Engine Company of Leeds, who took over the good-will of the locomotives business formerly carried out by Avonside, which ceased operations in 1931.

The "dock road" locomotives always aroused interest or amusement among passers-by when they ventured among the people and traffic along the stretch of roadway that crossed the Pier Head area, between Princes and Canning Docks. As the train reached each street intersection, men carrying red and green flags descended from the locomotive, walked into the centre of the roadway and waved the traffic to a standstill, cars, lorries, trams and buses drew to a halt while the engine accelerated with lusty exhaust blasts, its bell tolling with each revolution of the wheels and the wagons trailing behind it. Motor drivers inched their vehicles forward as the tail of the train drew near and with the impatience which is characteristic of so many drivers, the traffic was on the move again as the train cleared the crossing, barely missing the buffers of the last wagon!

The MD & HB engines were always kept clean, and even though painted black, looked smart with their red side-rods and polished brass domes, whilst every other piece of brass and copperwork was also polished. In 1953 the livery was changed to a pleasing shade of green. An example of a "dock road" engine in this colour scheme can be seen in the Transport Gallery of the Merseyside County Museum in Liverpool, in which MD & HB locomotive No. 1 stands at rest after half-a-century of service along the docks. Very many thanks indeed are due to the late Mersey Docks & Harbour Board for their splendid gesture of preserving this priceless treasure and representative of a locomotive design, the neat appearance of which matched its usefulness.

Characteristic features of the "dock road" locomotives were the spark-arresting chimneys with wire mesh netting to deflect sparks that might otherwise escape, and the hinged baffle fitted to divert smoke and steam from rising into the girders of the Overhead Railway. Each locomotive was equipped with a heavy brass bell, which was fitted onto a stretcher between the frames and, worked by a rocker arm from the connecting rod. This tolled continuously as the engine travelled. Archaic regulations required this fitting.

The whistle on the Avonside engines was an effective scream, similar in tone to the whistles on the locomotives of France and Holland. The whistle was mounted on the steam dome and was worked by a cord from the footplate, this being strung out above the top of the tank like a clothes line. The Hunslet engines had a deep-tone whistle, more like a hooter. In order to permit the locomotives to negotiate severe curves, the centre coupled wheels were flangeless.

On a bracket at the rear of the engine's coal bunker there usually rested a shovel with a short cranked steel shaft. This was used for fire and smokebox cleaning purposes, and was so designed that it could be easily manipulated in the narrow confines of the footplate and firebox. The ordinary firing shovel also had a short shaft, and when not in use was sometimes stuck, blade downwards between the saddle tank and hand-rail. The firebox on these engines was so small that firing them was quite like throwing coal into a household grate!

For work around the oil installations at Herculaneum Dock, two 0-6-0 Fireless locomotives were employed. These were charged periodically from a boiler specially installed at the south end of Herculaneum No. 1 Graving Dock through pipes laid to the engine shed at the Oil Depot. The receivers on the engines were charged to a pressure of 160 pounds per square inch, the locomotives returning for a fresh charge when pressure had fallen to 20 pounds per square inch. One of the Fireless engines, No. 44 received a direct hit during an air-raid in 1940 and was completely destroyed. The other, No. 43 lasted in use until early 1969, and was then sold.

When MD & HB locomotives required heavy repairs, they went to the Avonside Engine Company in Bristol, but when that company ceased business in 1931, engines were sent to the Hunslet Engine Company in Leeds, who took over the good-will of Avonside. During World War II, the London, Midland & Scottish Railway, carried out heavy repairs to several bomb-damaged engines at Crewe and Horwich.

Repairs of a smaller nature were carried out by Messrs Adair & Company, who tendered for the work on engines Nos 2 and 3 in June 1909. They had premises at 23 Waterloo Road, 2 Sligo Street and 22 Dundee Street, and carried on doing locomotive repairs for the MD & HB until about 1939.

In 1934 engines Nos. 22 and 39 were repaired by Grayson, Rollo & Clover Docks Ltd, but this was exceptional. The MD & HB built a repair works at Princes Dock in 1940 and subsequently carried out locomotive overhauls themselves.

Repainting of locomotives was done for a time by F. W. Wheatley & Company, nearby paint manufacturers who had premises at 50 Regent Road and Fulton Street. Engines were green until 1927 when the livery was changed to black. In 1953 however, green once again became the livery, but only a few locomotives were so painted. Three coats of paint and two coats of varnish were applied at a cost of £29 per engine in 1927. Incidentally, the museum-piece, engine No. 1, finished its service in black and was painted green for preservation. Its brass dome is not characteristic however, as the domes were painted over many years ago.

The MD & HB steam locomotives dwindled away one-by-one in the post-war years as new diesel locomotives were introduced, so that by 1965 or so, only about half-a-dozen remained. The last use of steam, and then only intermittently, was on the South Docks up to the middle of 1966, and it was pleasant indeed to see the lone steam lcomotive among the diesels, which themselves were destined to have less and less work to do in the coming years.

The dockside lines were a stronghold of steam until the year 1944 when a diesel-mechanical locomotive, built by the Hunslet Engine Company, Leeds was obtained for trials, and stayed on the job. This engine, of the 0-6-0 type, became No. 32 in the fleet, taking the number formerly borne by an Avonside Saddle Tank which had been sold some years previously. It was seven years before another diesel appeared — No. 34, another Hunslet 0-6-0, and the reign of steam came to the beginning of its demise. Further diesel-mechanical 0-6-0 locomotives were obtained during the 1950's and early 1960's, from Hudswell Clarke & Company of Leeds, and these were numbered 34 to 42 and 44 to 47.

Apart from the regular MD & HB locomotives, others were hired at times of pressure, such as during the war years, when several strangers appeared on the Liverpool dock lines. In January 1941 two large 0-6-0 Side Tank engines were hired from the Port of London Authority — Nos. 38 and 61. They returned to their home railway in September 1945.

In addition to the PLA locomotives just mentioned, five United States Army 0-6-0 Tank engines of the wartime Standard design were put to work on the Liverpool dock lines in 1943. They were USA Nos. 1304, 1313, 1967, 4396 and 4400. These engines belonged to the US Army Transportation Corps and several hundreds of them came to Britain in readiness for the European invasion, then in the planning stage. Most of the engines were placed in storage but a number were hired out to works and colliery lines. They were (with few exceptions) sent to the continent eventually. Many of the engines were off-loaded from ships in Liverpool docks and hauled away to storage bases coupled into goods trains. Those used on the docks here were returned to the USA authorities late in 1944.

The Esso Petroleum Co. Ltd employed two ex-MD & HB 0-6-0 diesel shunting locomotives at the Dingle Oil Depot until it closed in 1976. One of these was then sent to work at Milford Haven refinery, whilst the other ended up at Hull. They went away on road transporter vehicles.

Finally, it remains to be mentioned that the MD & HB employed several really ancient engines for pumping work. Mainly, they came from the L & NW and L & Y Railways and among the former were several from the Liverpool & Manchester Railway which the L & NWR disposed of soon after taking them over in 1846. The last survivor of those old engines was the ex-L & M 0-4-2 "Lion", which finished work at Princes Dock in 1928 after 90 years driving a pump. Fortunately it was rescued and restored and is now a resident of the Liverpool Museum in William Brown Street. Steam locomotives can certainly last for a long time! "Lion", built by Todd, Kitson & Laird of Leeds in 1838, is now 153 years old and is still in working order, making many trips out to various railway functions where it has become as familiar as many much younger preserved locomotives.

As mentioned earlier, the main-line railway companies worked trains along the dock railway between their own goods depots, all of which were on the landward side of the dock road. None of the company-owned engines ventured into the dock estate which was strictly the preserve of the MD & HB locomotives. Taking the London Midland & Scottish Railway first, the usual engines were the tiny 0-4-0 Saddle Tanks from the former L & Y and which were known as "Pugs". These worked on the docks from 1895 until the early 1960's, complete with smoke baffles and continuously tolling bells. Another, larger L & Y class was the Aspinall 0-6-0 Side Tank employed mainly at Bankfield depot but often made a dock road trip to the LMS (ex-L & NWR) Canada Dock goods station. The L & NWR used quaint 0-4-0 Saddle Tank engines on the dock road, these, known ar the 2ft 6in shunters, were replaced by the "Pugs" after the 1923 Grouping, and thereafter were confined to the Alexandra and Canada goods yards for work in the sections of the yards with very sharp curves.

Not to be left out, the Cheshire Lines Committee used London & North Eastern Railway engines between Brunswick yard and the Great Central depot at Canada Dock. These were Great Central design 0-6-0 Side Tank engines of L & NER Class J63. After the Great Central depot was destroyed by bombing in 1940, this working ceased. It was strange to see engines of a predominently east coast railway on the docks of a west coast port!

Commencing in 1960, British Railways brought in some small 0-4-0 diesel-hydraulic locomotives to replace the old steam "Pugs", but it was an expensive exercise because most of the dock road work disappeared during the 1960's and they became redundant. A few remained in use within the Alexandra and Canada Dock goods stations until the early 1970's.

Finally, a novel use for locomotives was the testing of bridges. For instance, on 1st December 1906, the then new bowstring girder bridge at Queen's Dock was tested by running several locomotives across together, and also standing them still on the span. Present were three MD & HB Avonside 0-6-0 Saddle tanks, two L & NWR 0-4-0 Saddle Tanks and one L & NWR 0-4-2- "Bissell Truck" Saddle Tank, the latter being a type that did not normally work on the dock road.

So ends the story of steam locomotives on the dock streets of Liverpool. They were one of the sights of the city for 65 years or so and were greatly missed — no longer the fragrant coal smoke beneath the Overhead Railway (which that company did not appreciate), the steady tolling of the warning bell and the thrilling experience among small boys of being able to stand close to an engine at track-level, sniff the aroma of hot oil and feel its warmth on a cold day — a pleasant memory indeed!

The character of Dockland is well portrayed in this view of MD&HB Avonside 0-6-0 Saddle Tank No. 10 and its crew. June 1957. Photo — F. Jones

MD&HB Hunslet 0-6-0 Saddle Tank at Nelson Dock. May 1960.
Photo — T. Taylor

MD&HB 0-6-0 Diesel locomotive No. 41 at Canada Dock, August 1973.
Photo — J.A. Peden

MD&HB Diesel No. 35 hauling oil tank wagons near Brunswick Dock. May 1959.   Photo — J. Feild

"Pug" No. 51237 crossing Blackstone Street, Liverpool in October 1959.
Photo — S. Williams

British Railways ex-L&Y "Pug" 0-4-0 Saddle Tank No. 51206, a regular dock road engine, seen at Great Howard Street in November, 1960.
Photo — J.F. Ward

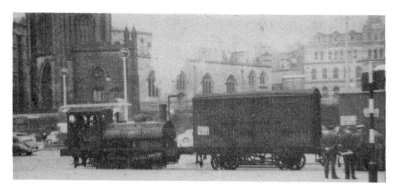

A "Pug" No. 51237 trundles past Liverpool Parish Church of St. Nicholas with a train of banana vans in 1958. Photo — M. Jenkins

CHAPTER FOUR (Part Two)

Rolling Stock

For internal use on the Liverpool dock estate, the Mersey Docks & Harbour Board had a stock of about 220 open coal wagons which were mostly used by the Engineering Department, and low-sided wagons for carrying timber. Wagons could be hired by anyone desiring to move materials along the docks.

Most, if not all the wagons were obtained second-hand. For instance, in 1923, 20 single-bolster wagons and ten open wagons were obtained via Captain George Davison, whilst a number of wagons of ex-North Eastern Railway stock were purchased from the London & North Eastern Railway Company. In 1928 six single-bolster wagons and 20 low-sided open wagons were purchased from York via Captain Davison.

In 1934 a number of old wagons were sold for scrap to Messrs Maden & McKee. More went to that firm in 1936. Some wagons were sold to the Standard Railway Wagon Company Ltd in 1937. More wagons went for scrap in 1938 to J. Routledge & Sons and T. W. Ward Ltd.

In 1939 one hundred high-sided open wagons were obtained from Evesons (Coal) Ltd, extra sidings being laid on Muspratt's Estate at Seaforth to accommodate them.

Many MD & HB wagons came from collieries, some from Parkend Colliery in the Forest of Dean, the name of which could be seen plainly as the overpainted red livery of the MD & HB weathered away! Many older wagons had dumb buffers, probably the last surviving vehicles with such in the Liverpool area. Dumb buffers were banned from the main line railways in 1913! There was no compulsion however to abolish dumb buffers on wagons used within the confines of works or docks etc.

The MD & HB wagons were mostly kept on the field at Seaforth Sands, which was a works and graveyard combined. Repairs were carried out here, though many wagons that stood in the sidings were beyond salvation after the Second World War, being in an advanced state of decrepitude. Nevertheless, there was a sound fleet of vehicles ready for use. In the late 1960's most of these wagons were sold or scrapped, some being taken away on motor lorries.

Railway companies, and later BR wagons, were used for normal traffic of course, and until recent times a stock of about 1,500 "Common User" wagons was always present on the dock estate. In the final years a few dozen was the most one was likely to find! Some past figures are of interest — in 1908 10,066 loaded wagons were dealt with at the Liverpool docks. In 1929 the figure was 154,374 loaded wagons.

Coaching stock and vehicles with a long wheelbase were banned from working onto the Liverpool docks except for the line between Waterloo Dock and Riverside station. Many long-wheelbase vans carried the inscription "Not To Be Loaded to the Mersey Dock Estate". The ban was, of course, due to the exceptionally sharp curves encountered on the dock lines. No large locomotives were allowed either, so that 0-6-0 Tank engines with a short wheelbase were the only engines used within the dock estate.

In 1988 the only railway vehicles to be seen, on the North docks only, are Freightliner container wagons for the Royal Seaforth Dock traffic, occasional "Railfreight" wagons with export steel through Hornby Dock, and condemned wagons going to the steel shearing plant at the Seaforth end of the estate.

British Railways ex-L&Y "Pug" 0-4-0 Saddle Tank No. 51206 crossing James Street, Liverpool in 1954, beneath the Liverpool Overhead Railway,
Photo — J.F. Ward collection

Ex-L&Y "Pug" No. 51206 on the High-level Coal Railway at Bramley-Moore Dock, 1959.
Photo — J.A. Peden

British Railways, ex-L&Y 0-6-0 Tank engine No. 51537 at Bankfield Yard in November, 1960. This class worked along the dock road only between Canada and North Mersey.
Photo — J.F. Ward

Freightliner from Seaforth to Garston about to cross the main dock road near Alexandra Dock, to run via the Bootle Branch to Edge Hill. Class 47 Locomotive. July, 1983. Photo — S.G. Jones

Ex-LMS 2-6-4 Tank No. 42613 propels a Brake Van along Beaufort Road, Birkenhead Docks in February 1967. Photo — R.L. Wilson

CHAPTER FIVE

Birkenhead and Wallasey

The system of docks in Birkenhead and Wallasey is entirely different from that on the Liverpool side of the Mersey, where they are strung in a line along the bank of the river. On the Cheshire side the nucleus of the docks system was the tidal creek or inlet from the Mersey known as Wallasey Pool which provided a ready-made haven which only needed deepening and quays constructed on its banks. The Pool was the outlet of a marsh that once extended right across the Wirral Peninsula at its north western extremity, and schemes for the development of the Pool as a port were aired from time to time. Indeed, a canal through to the River Dee was proposed in 1828 by the engineers Thomas Telford, Robert Stephenson and Alexander Nimmo, but nothing came of this.

Between 1818 and 1824, William Laird and Sir John Tobin purchased from Francis Price, land adjacent to the Pool for the purpose of building docks, but the Liverpool Council, alarmed at the prospect of a rival dock system also bought land near the Pool and River Mersey, so no work on the proposed docks was carried out, and the land lay idle for a number of years.

By the early 1840's, the Liverpool Corporation no longer wishing to retain the land, put it up for sale, thus opening up the possibility for the docks project to be revived, this time by the Birkenhead Town Commissioners. They soon formed a company to manage the construction and operation of docks, led by Sir John Laird, son of William who had died in 1841.The Liverpool Council objected of course, but to no avail. Their action in selling the land opened up the way for formidable competition to their own Liverpool docks.

An Act of Parliament authorising the construction of docks in Birkenhead was passed on 9th July 1844. The foundation stone of the first dock was laid with due ceremony on 23rd October of that year by Sir Philip Egerton, the proceedings being accompanied by military bands and the formal booming of canon. It was a gala day for Birkenhead and the future looked bright. The new docks were built under the supervision of J. M. Rendel. Many difficulties were encounterd before and after completion including the collapse of the river wall, which was actually a temporary dam across the mouth of the Pool seven years after the docks were opened. Rendel was eventually replaced by James Abernethy, whilst the great

Birkenhead contractor Thomas Brassey worked on rebuilding the dam, together with Rendel who had been reinstated. They were unsuccessful however and the construction of locks to enable ships to enter or leave the docks was undertaken by others. Meanwhile entrance and exit was via the Woodside basin. In later years improvements were carried out by Jesse Hartley of the Mersey Docks & Harbour Board, after that body had assumed responsibility for the dock systems on either side of the river, of which more later.

The first two docks, Morpeth and Egerton, were opened amid great rejoicing and festivity, by Lord Morpeth, on Easter Monday, 5th April 1847. On the same day the Birkenhead, Lancashire & Cheshire Junction Railway Company opened the line from Grange Lane to Canning Street which served the new docks. A train of coal, mined at Ruabon early that day, arrived at Canning Street, where the locomotive was detached, the wagons then being hauled by horses onto the quayside alongside the paddle steamer "Lord Warden", into the bunkers of which the coal was loaded for fuel. The steamer then took distinguished persons on a voyage round the docks. This ship had been built in Laird's yard nearby. In dock that day was another vessel, the "Oregon" with a cargo of guano, this unpleasant substance being transferred into railway wagons and a train made up, which was immediately despatched to Chester in order to demonstrate the quickness of rail transit from the new docks.

In 1848 the Commissioners, who had not done too well in their administration, were replaced by Dock Trustees. This body were ambitious, and went so far as to purchase the Herculaneum Dock in Liverpool. Alas, they too were unequal to their task and sold the entire Birkenhead Dock Estate to the Liverpool Corporation. This took place in 1855. The days of Corporation administration of both Liverpool and Birkenhead docks were by then numbered however, for an Act of Parliament passed on 25th August 1857 created the Mersey Dock & Harbour Board to control the construction and management of all docks on both sides of the river. The board existed until 31st July 1971 after which it was replaced by the present Mersey Docks & Harbour Company.

After part of Wallasey Pool had been transformed into docks, it became known as the Great Float, and after further quays and docks had been built, of which more later, it was divided into two sections — East Float and West Float, which names still apply today.

Not only did William Laird dream of a vast docks complex back in the 1820's, but he also visualised Birkenhead becoming a splendid "city of the future" with long, wide streets laid out on the grid pattern, lined with beautiful houses and shops. Lack of finance prevented much being done in this direction, the magnificent Hamilton Square being an example of what was intended and which was fortunately completed. Of the wide thoroughfares only Cleveland Street and Conway Street were made, but the grid pattern is discernable in the streets in between these two. Docks and industry meant houses for workers so instead of the fine city, Birkenhead became covered with narrow streets of terraced dwellings, industrial premises and gas works. Birkenhead did however have the first municipal park, opened on the same day as the first docks.

The first railway lines were laid on the Birkenhead Dock Estate in 1847, and the greater part of the subsequently extensive system was laid during the following 16 years. The network became extensive, rails penetrating into almost every nook and corner, and unlike the situation at Liverpool where the dock lines were semi-reserved, those at Birkenhead passed in tramway fashion along the centre of public roads. The earliest track had keyed joints, and some examples of this survived until World War II. A considerable variety of track construction was employed due to the different surfaces, so that rails were laid in cobblestones, setts, concrete, tarmac and in the ordinary open way on timber sleepers. The junctions were numerous and some were of a complex nature, whilst many different kinds of rail were employed. Indeed, much of the history of rails, from early iron examples to the much more modern could be found on the Birkenhead Dock Estate.

The following notes must necessarily refer to the past, around 1947 or so, when the docks were still busy and rail traffic still intensive, because, since the end of World War II, traffic has slowly ebbed away and vast dereliction has resulted. It was only during the 1980's that plans for redevelopment of the disused areas of the dock estate have been made and now in progress, whilst some new industrial concerns have moved into the dock area in recent times. Some spasmodic rail traffic survives however, which will be mentioned later on.

The peculiar layout of Birkenhead and Wallasey docks makes a straightforward description somewhat difficult. A "circular tour" would appear to be the best method of exploration, commencing at Shore Road near the Woodside Ferry stage, thence following the various roads and wharves, and after an arduous walk of several miles, arrive back at the starting point. So, to turn the clock back as we did for the Liverpool tour, we arrive at the Woodside end of Shore Road, wearing strong boots, for the going will get quite hard!

An imposing gatehouse in weathered sandstone, bearing the date 1868, guards the entrance to Shore Road. This thoroughfare is of considerable length and is paved with granite setts on the portion for road traffic, whilst on the east side run three parallel railway tracks laid in setts or cobblestones with crossover connections at frequent intervals. Upon passing through the gates we see the extensive cattle sheds for imported animals on the right-hand side, with rail lines passing through the entrances, whilst on the left-hand side stands the Mersey Railway electric power station with its 280-foot chimney. A sharply-curved single-line spur from the "main line" runs into the power station so that wagons bringing coal for its fuel can reach the bunkers. Shore Road tracks were re-laid in 1889 with steel rails to replace the original iron rails, and again re-laid in 1927. In the latter year, a second line into the Mersey Railway premises was removed.

The three main tracks mentioned earlier run the full length of Shore Road, and branches lead off into the long dockside transit sheds. Beyond the Mersey Railway power station lies the extensive goods station, built by the Cheshire Lines Committee, which was opened in July 1871 and extended in 1889.

On the right-hand side of the road, hidden from view by transit sheds, is Morpeth Dock together with a smaller branch dock. These are mainly used nowadays as berths for idle ships. Vessels of the Isle of Man Steam Packet Company spend the winter here, whilst Mersey ferry steamers, tugs and dredgers are laid up when not in use.

In a corner of the Cheshire Lines Committee's goods yard there is a small engine shed which is at the west end of Shore Road. This shed, formerly owned by the Cheshire Lines Committee, accommodates several locomotives which are employed by J. Perrin & Sons, the transport contractors. At this juncture it should be noted that nowadays the Mersey Docks & Harbour Board do not perform any rail haulage on Birkenhead Dock Estate as they did formerly, even though they own all the track with the exception of a small amount at East Float and Cathcart Street wharf. All shunting is now carried out by the main-line railway companies and local contractors.

Turning to the right at the end of Shore Road, a large steel bascule lifting bridge is reached. This structure spans the water passage between Morpeth and Egerton Docks, over which the railway passes to fan out into the large marshalling yard on land known as the South Reserve. On this are situated Morpeth Dock goods station and Manchester Sidings. The former originated with the Shrewsbury & Chester Railway Company in 1851, whilst the latter most likely take their name from the Birkenhead, Manchester & Cheshire Junction Railway, the original title of what became the Birkenhead, Lancashire & Cheshire Junction system. From Morpeth station, barges operated by the Great Western Company, took traffic over the Mersey to Liverpool, or to ships in the river (or in Liverpool docks). Great Western rails never succeeded in penetrating into Liverpool.

Shunting on the South Reserve is mainly performed by the familiar Great Western 0-6-0 Pannier Tank locomotives which are kept busy dealing with hundreds of wagons daily. The older engines with open-backed cabs are preferred on the docks, as the absence of a back-plate allows greater visibility for the crew, though less comfort. Visibility is an important factor where streets and dockside running is concerned. Engines nearing their time of withdrawal are sent to Birkenhead to complete their mileages on dock work, some coming from the Midlands, and as far distant as South-West Wales.

The main entrance to the South Reserve is on Tower Road, a stone sett-paved thoroughfare along which a double track runs, with many branches into industrial premises and docks etc. Trackwork is quite complicated in this locality, there being among other interesting formations two sets of three-way points side-by-side in the roadway! Trains mingle with road traffic in an intensively busy and fascinating area.

After exploring Morpeth Dock we retrace our steps a little and revert to the end of Shore Road. From here we proceed in an westerly direction and shortly reach a gated level-crossing, somewhat unusual in this area of railway lines running along busy public roadways. This crossing is controlled by a signal box of L & NWR origin, which bears on its nameboards the title "Canning Street North". Here the jointly-operated LMS (ex-L & NW) and Great Western goods branch from Grange Road enters the dock estate. The rails in the immediate vicinity of the signal box are laid in the usual way on a ballasted formation, as road traffic is not permitted to encroach upon them except at the level-crossing, which has a footbridge for pedestrians. From the enclosed area rails pass out into streets, including the already-mentioned Tower Road along which they pass in tramway fashion, paved with granite setts.

The Canning Street level-crossing was originally the subject of great controversy. Back in 1845 it was proposed to raise Canning Street so as to cross the railway by a bridge, but owing to the heavy cost of such works the L & NWR received Parliamentary sanction for a level-crossing. This was objected to by the Board of Trade, but eventually, in 1869, the crossing was made at the joint expense of the London & North Western and Great Western companies, the Corporation of Birkenhead and the Mersey Docks & Harbour Board.

The line which passes over the level-crossing is the double-track main line which runs from this location to the furthest point of the dock estate where it connects with the lines of the LMS, formerly Wirral Railway. Lengthy trains use this line so the gates and signal box are necessary. Trains run under normal signalling between Canning Street and the main Birkenhead-Chester line at Grange Road.

From the level-crossing we next proceed in a westerly direction along Corporation Road, which is a mixed residential and industrial thoroughfare, built-up on its south side, with the docks on the north side and the "main line" of the docks railway behind a high brick wall on the latter side of the street. Tantalising sounds of locomotives are heard as one proceeds and passes the Vittoria Dock goods depot which is behind the agravating wall, but a gateway about half-way along gives a glimpse inside, whilst a little further on there is a level-crossing opposite the end of Marcus Street which allows traffic to and from the Mersey Tunnel and Docks to cross the railway. Vittoria Dock was opened in 1909, but a quay named Vittoria Wharf was opened much earlier, in 1861. In the 1860's a fantastic amount of railway track in wondrous configurations was provided at Vittoria and Egerton Docks, with many wagon turntables to allow access to sheds etc. In later years the rail layout was simplified and most of the turntables abolished.

The long brick wall ends at the intersection of Corporation Road and Duke Street — an amazing and intensely interesting place indeed, where a policeman on duty in a sort of pulpit directs both road vehicles and trains! Here are very busy main roads with the "main line" crossing Duke Street without any protecting gates, with tracks branching off and passing along the centre of the thoroughfare. Ahead, an extensive array of sidings fans out from the main line alongside the West Float, with Corporation Road continuing alongside the railway, but now with only a low wall which does not obscure the view!

On the West Float side is Duke Street wharf at which there are several coal tips and coaling berths. Here too scrap metal is exported, much of it arriving by rail and several locomotives are kept busy shunting wagons on the extensive wharf sidings.

The rails running along Duke Street cross the passage between the East and West Floats by a large steel lifting bridge in order to reach the Wallasey side of the Great Float (the division between Birkenhead and Wallasey is the exact centre of the waterway). This street track and the first bridge, which was a plate-girder swing bridge, were installed in 1861. The present bridge was opened on 4th

March 1931. After installation it was tested by two steam locomotives being run across — a GWR Class 56XX 0-6-2 Tank and an LMS (ex-L & NW) 0-8-0. An LNER engine intended to take part was unable to reach the bridge through its wheels binding tightly on the sharp curves.

Continuing along Corporation Road we next pass Cavendish Wharf sidings and presently reach the junction with Patten Street, where a disused single-line branch veers from the main line and crosses Corporation Road at an angle to reach an iron foundry. Here too, the double-track line of the Birkenhead Corporation Tramways crossed this branch, the actual crossings being still in place even though the tram route concerned (Line of Docks) was converted to bus operation in April 1935.

Proceeding onwards it is necessary to bear to the right into Beaufort Road in order to follow the railway. The double-track docks "main line" still runs alongside the roadway but is not walled off — it simply runs along the verge. Branches and sidings serve dockside wharves, industrial premises and Rank's Ocean flour mills. About here there was once an inlet from the Pool, from which was formed the present Gillbrook Basin. It was here that William Laird opened his first shipbuilding yard and iron foundry in 1824, and from the yard was launched the first iron ship in 1829. Laird's establishment was known as "Paddy's Yard", presumably due to the large number of Irishmen employed there. The shipbuilding business was transferred to Tranmere on the bank of the Mersey during the 1850's. His iron foundry at Gillbrook basin was provided with a rail connection in 1862.

A little distance beyond Gillbrook Basin there are three graving docks, and the site of a former inlet which was named Canada Creek. Here was established, in 1855, the famous Canada Works of Messrs Peto, Betts & Brassey, who got the contract for building the Canadian Grand Trunk Railway — everything including locomotives being built here and shipped out. Among the tasks involved was the construction of Victoria Bridge at Montreal, which was two miles in length and took from 1854 to 1858 to complete. The Canada Works was rail-served from the line on Beaufort Road. Unfortunately, the Canada Works, which became The Canada Works Engineering & Shipbuilding Company closed in 1889 and no trace of it now remains.

Presently, after a fairly long walk, we come to Wharf Road which runs to the Float and has rail lines, and a little distance further-on we arrive at the corner of Waliasey Bridge Road. The railway passes over this busy thoroughfare by a gated level-crossing, the gates being opened and closed by train crews as there is no signal box. On the West side of Wallasey Bridge Road is the complex of buildings that form the LMS Railway electric car sheds and repair depot which were opened in 1938 to service trains on the Wirral electric lines. There was formerly a steam locomotive depot here known as Birkenhead North, originally built by the Wirral Railway Company, and also a goods and coal depot.

The first section of the Wirral Railway was opened in 1863 and was originally named the Hoylake Railway. Its terminus was at this location. The company became bankrupt after only a few troubled years and was taken over in 1872 by the Hoylake & Birkenhead Rail & Tramway Company, which as well as operating the railway also ran a service of horse-drawn trams to Birkenhead via Beaufort Road, Corporation Road and Cleveland Street.

Wishing to run goods trains, the H & BR & T Company asked the Mersey Docks & Harbour Board to allow them to make a junction with the dock railway. Before any agreement was made, the Hoylake company put in a connection and worked traffic into the docks. This happened early in 1878. The MD & HB objected to the practice of course, but in August of that year allowed the use of their lines at a charge of one shilling per wagon, which was later increased to two shillings. The lines used were on Beaufort Road, and a stop-block was provided at the junction, which was unlocked by a watchman who kept a record of all wagons passing from and to the Hoylake line. A permit had to be applied for by the Hoylake company for every movement over the dock lines, but in 1880 the MD & HB withdrew the permit system and allowed the Hoylake company to pay monthly and themselves keep a record of the traffic.

The tramway section of the H & BR & T Company was transferred to the Corporation of Birkenhead in 1879, but in 1881 a new company, the Seacombe, Hoylake & Deeside Railway took over the line to Hoylake. The title Wirral Railway dates from June 1891.

In order to reach the north side of the docks, we next turn into Wallasey Bridge Road, which has a large oil depot on its east side, served by a double track railway line. This installation was originally established by the Anglo-American Oil Company before the turn of the century. The next item of interest is a single line which crosses the road and enters a gateway on the left, after which it throws off branches and sidings. On the west side of the road there are further sidings, and beyond them Bidston Moss stretches away, whilst a glance to the south reveals the wooded slopes of Bidston Hill, presenting a pleasing picture. Presently a gateway on the left is reached, and through this a single line of rails emerges at an angle and curves to pass along the centre of the roadway. It is laid with grooved tramway-type rails, in stone setts, and passes over Poulton bridge, a steel Bascule structure which was built by Francis Morton & Company, Liverpool, and bears the date 1926. This bridge crosses the passage linking Bidston Dock with West Float. Bidston Dock was opened in 1933 but, of course, the creek out of which the Float was developed flowed well west of Poulton Bridge Road. A swing bridge was built at this location in 1842, and as a charge of One Penny was made to everyone crossing it, the structure became known as the "Penny Bridge". This toll lasted as late as 1937, being applied on the present bridge until that date. Indeed, even in the the 1990's people still refer to the "Penny Bridge"!

Bidston Dock is rail-served, the track along the street enabling trains to reach the north quay — it curves to the left after running for some distance along the road on the north side of Poulton bridge. Here the road is named Poulton Bridge Road and the residential district of Poulton borders onto the dock estate. Near the intersection of Poulton Bridge Road with Dock Road a single track crosses the street. This runs from the north quay of Bidston Dock to an oil depot, then onwards to the quays of West Float. Proceeding a little further onwards, just before reaching the junction with Dock Road a level crossing is arrived at, and at this point the Slopes Branch enters the dock estate. This double track line, which was opened in 1906, leaves the LMS Wirral line at Slopes Branch Junction signal box on the Bidston-Seacombe section, and passes between houses to emerge at Poulton Bridge Road level crossing. The branch was named after a house called "The Slopes", which no longer exists.

An array of large storage tanks, some for oil and others for molasses border the roadway in this area, whilst there are also various industrial premises served by the railway. Proceeding in a generally easterly direction, the junction of Limekiln Lane with Dock Road is reached. These two roads merge near the complex of buildings that form the Wallasey gas and electric works. The gas works originated as long ago as 1860, but the electric power station is much newer — it replaced an earlier works which was in Seaview Road. The newer station was opened in 1914. Until World War II both works had their own railway wagons for transporting their fuel supplies, but during and after the war railway-owned wagons were used, due firstly to the wartime pooling of vehicles, and later the abolition of privately-owned mineral wagons.

The docks "main line" runs on its own reservation right through to Tower Road near Seacombe. Some curious and intricate examples of trackwork are characteristic of this stretch of railway, one in particular near the gas and electricity works. This consists of the double-track main line, a double track crossing it at right-angles and adjacent to this a scissors crossing, all the rails being laid in stone setts. Reduced wartime maintenance resulted in the whole lot sinking, so that at times of heavy rain the roadway becomes flooded. When a train passes over the crossings the engine pitches like a ship in a storm, the wagons bouncing along behind it — a fascinating spectacle indeed! (The junction was simplified and re-laid at a later date). A branch line runs into the gas and electricity works here.

On the south side of Dock Road, spurs and sidings serve goods sheds on the bank of the West Float, the whole area being busy with both rail and road traffic. To the left lie the Wallasey Mills and a refuse destructor, each with its own railway lines, whilst on the right-hand side of the road looms the extensive, high, busy mills of Spillers Ltd. A few-minutes walk onwards brings us to the intersection of Gorsey Lane, Duke Street and Dock Road, after passing the East and West Float goods station which was opened in November 1892 by the Cheshire Lines Committee. This lies on the north side of the road, two lines crossing the highway to connect the depot with the docks railway. At the intersection of the aforementioned roads, railway lines branch into Duke Street. There is also a considerable amount of old abandoned track from early years remaining in the cobblestones at the sides of the roads, which was supplanted by new track as dock extensions and alterations were carried out. The rails running along Duke Street cross a steel bascule bridge which spans the passage linking the East and West Floats.

On the east side of Gorsey Lane, at Creekside (named after the former "Creek House") there is another goods station which was built by the London & North Western and Great Western Railways, the spur line serving this having been originally built to reach brick works and other long-vanished premises. The site occupied by the goods depot was, from 1903, the location of a large steel works owned by the English McKenna Process Company, which was served by a branch from the dock railway, and had its own locomotive. Unfortunately the steel works had only a short life, the company going into liquidation in 1911 and the whole complex was demolished. The office building still survives however, being entitled "McKenna Building".

Continuing onwards, we enter a busy industrial area of enormous, grim-looking grain mills and warehouses which stretch for quite a long distance, being owned by Buchanan's, Spillers, Vernons, Paul Bros. and the Liverpool Grain Storage and Transit Co. Numerous railway tracks accompany the roadway, with branches running to the quays of the East Float, and also to various industrial premises. Here the open and spacious nature of the scene changes abruptly as the dark canyon-like narrow area between the looming mills is entered. These mill buildings range from the 1860's to fairly modern, with some parts rebuilt after heavy war damage, and they rear their enormous bulk either side of the roadway, shutting out the sunshine for most of the day. Railway lines penetrate through these mills and cross the road at right-angles from one building to another. Large motor lorries pass to and fro, and lines of railway bulk-grain vans stand on the sidings adjacent to the mills. Shunting engines are busy, whilst motor traffic is also heavy and frequent. Buses too, pass through the area — the blue ones of Birkenhead and the yellow vehicles of Wallasey Corporation. There are not many places at which a bus can pass a train in the street, but it is quite normal in this district!

Beyond the "canyon" formed by the enormous buildings comprising the grain mills and warehouses, Dock Road is joined by Oakfield Road on its north side, but on the south side of Dock Road a range of high, gloomy grain warehouses stretch for some considerable distance, all the buildings being ancient, dating from the year 1868 and in design are quite similar to those at Waterloo Dock, Liverpool. On the north side of the Dock Road various small industrial premises are served by single line branches from the "main line" which cross the roadway to enter yards or buildings. Lines and sidings continue along in front of the aforementioned warehouses, and a single line spur crosses Dock Road to reach the goods station at Kelvin Road, which was built by the Great Central Railway and opened in October 1906. Kelvin Road is part industrial and part residential, and is crossed by a double line which runs from the goods station to the premises of Messers Currie, Rowlands & Co Ltd, fertilizer manufacturers, who have their own locomotive. From these works a single line runs out across Birkenhead Road and joins the docks railway again near Dock Road. Here there is a spacious area of wide roads, numerous railway lines, some on reservations. Curves lead round to Birkenhead Road and also southwards towards the Great Float, with complicated trackwork in the roadway. Opposite this busy area is Alfred Dock, which was opened in 1866.

Birkenhead Road runs from this point to Seacombe Ferry, its West side being lined by red-brick houses, shops and industrial premises. A double line, on its own reservation runs along the east side of the road, this line having been built chiefly for coal traffic and runs to Seacombe Ferry stage. Indeed, coal for the steamers was delivered here, and there were several coal merchants yards along the road. In October 1872 Mr Meyrick Banks received permission to lay a track from the main line crossing the road to reach his yard, which was on the west side. The next year the following obtained leave from the MD&HB to use the lines to Seacombe: Messers Thomas Longrigg & Co; J.P.Higginson & Co; The North Western Coal & Cannel Co; William Sumner; The Wallasey Local Board; Meyrick Banks; Edward McGeoch; Messers R. Brewin & Co. Others followed over the years. It would appear that the lines to the Ferry yard from Birkenhead Road, completed in 1880 were laid by the Wallasey Local Board.

In 1882 Messers T.R & J.J Nickson, whose premises were on the west side of Birkenhead Road, were using locomotives to haul their traffic. They sold out to Lee & Robinson in 1885, who were shunting contractors, the business later being taken over by William J. Lee. Another shunting contractor on Birkenhead Road was Rowland Owen & Sons, whose depot was on the west side, but they ceased business shortly after the end of World War II.

Until 1887 there were small shipbuilding yards along the shore on the east side of Birkenhead Road, the first one commencing in 1864 to an ultimate total of five, but not all in business simultaneously. Part of the foreshore here was claimed from the river

On the east, or riverward, side of Birkenhead Road there is an extensive area of open land known as "Scotts Field", but to the dock authority it is the "North Reserve". This land is used as an "attic" or storage dump for a great variety of plant. Old boilers, cranes, carts, railway wagons, motor vehicles and a host of mechanical bits and pieces stand in the long grass and weeds. There are a number of very ancient side-tipping railway wagons with dumb buffers, dating back to the 1850's, which see occasional use! The land is kept separate from the public road by a sleeper fence.

We follow the line to Seacombe, which was laid in 1866, and soon reach the busy coal depot with its sidings and spur tracks near Seacombe Ferry. A fairly wide, cobblestoned road called East Street runs from the coal depot towards the Alfred Dock entrance locks. The rails curve into this street and pass along the centre for some distance, with branches striking off to enter land on either side, once the scene of industrial activity including the shipbuilding yards mentioned earlier, but now the MD&HB yard. The seldom-used rails are of a very light section and are laid in the cobblestones without any check-rail.

At the north end of Birkenhead Road, just round the corner from the Seacombe Ferry and bus terminal, stop-blocks are affixed at the end of the double track and, until about 1938, a sharply-curved line led from the landward track across the road into a contractors yard at the corner of St. Paul's Road. This curve was not direct, leading off in a trailing direction only about a wagon-length from the buffers so that no locomotive could take a vehicle into the yard. Probably wagons were pushed up to the buffers one-at-a-time and hauled into the yard by a horse.

In earlier times the track at the Seacombe end of Birkenhead Road curved towards the river and, passing over a short bridge, ran onto the landing stage. Due to the fact that space was restricted, sidings were reached via turntables. Horse haulage was of course employed as locomotives could not be used because of the wagon-length turntables. The landing stage of that era was not, of course, a floating structure like that of later days.

At the Alfred Dock end of Birkenhead Road, on its east side near the junction with Dock Road is a small engine shed which was built in 1918 to house engines used by W. J. Lee, the shunting contractor.

We next proceed towards Birkenhead by passing along Tower Road, with the waters of the East Float on our right at a location known as "Mortar Mill Quay". Tower Road is notorious for its four opening bridges which try the tempers of motor drivers! Firstly we reach a steel rolling lift bridge which was built in 1931 to replace an older swing bridge spanning the passage linking Alfred Dock with the East Float. Almost adjacent is another bridge of swing type spanning a narrower passage between Alfred Dock and the Float. The double line railway crosses both bridges, trains mingling with road vehicles in a very unusual situation! A branch next curves away towards the Mersey, to serve the quays of Wallasey Dock, which was opened in 1877. This track runs along a thoroughfare entitled Pump Road, a name with hydraulic connotations.

A very prominent building claims attention in this locality — the Central Hydraulic Tower, which stands on Tower Road. This building, with its tall clock tower, is built in grey stonework and houses hydraulic machinery for operating dock gates, cranes etc. In appearence it resembles a cross between a monastery and a mediaeval castle! The front door, in appearence similar to that of a church, has a single track railway line passing through it to gain the interior of the building. Opened in 1863, the structure was designed by J.B. Hartley — son of the famous Jesse, the docks engineer. On entering the hydraulic tower, one steps back into the primeval age of mechanical history. The immense hydraulic rams present an awe-inspiring spectacle as they ascend and descend inside the tower, accommpanied by dripping water. The building was badly damaged during the air-raids of 1940, but was quickly patched up with

100

ordinary red bricks which spoils its appearençe, but aesthetic considerations don't apply in the middle of a war. (To digress from our period for a moment, the ornate openwork pinnacle was later removed leaving a castellated top to the tower). The picturesque tower occupies a cobblestoned area known as Tower Quay, on which lay several lines of very old track of light-section rail and incredibly sharp curves. This has not been used for many years as no modern locomotive or goods wagon could possibly negotiate the curved sections. Some of these lines served the East Float quays. Not far distant, on the quayside at the River Mersey end of Wallasey Dock, there is another hydraulic pumping station full of vintage machinery, white-tiled and lighted by gas (this was replaced by a new building with electrical plant but the old building housing the boilers remained).

To the south of the Central Hydrauliic Tower is yet another steel rolling lift bridge, which replaced an older swing bridge in 1932. This structure spans the passage between Wallasey Dock and the East Float. Branches from the "main line" in the street lead to the quayside of Wallasey Dock. Some of these railway lines are disused and have been for years, whilst others are very busy. A large open area on the riverward side of the road contains yet more railway sidings. Here the fourth bridge is reached — of the bascule lifting type, which was installed in 1932 to replace a hydraulic swing bridge that dated from 1886. Along the north side of Egerton Dock runs Spike Road, and further lines link up with those on the "South Reserve" mentioned earlier. The made-up land between Morpeth and Alfred Docks is referred to as "Spike Island", as it is reached only via bridges over waterways. Egerton Dock is on the riverward side beyond the last-mentioned bridge, and a little distance further on, we arrive at Shore Road where our tour began.

For the student of transport the Birkenhead and Wallasey docks provided tremendous interest. For instance, along Duke Street, passengers on buses can have a novel experience of seeing a goods train pass them travelling in the opposite direction, or the bus may overtake an engine on its way to pick up a train somewhere on the estate. This in itself is novel, but what is even more so is the sight of a locomotive among the lorries and cars queueing up to await an open bridge to close! (This still applied to a limited extent in 1988). The bridges of Birkenhead Docks often cause the blood pressure of vehicle drivers to rise due to these delays, their impatience contrasting with the calm demeanour of ships crews leaning over the rails gazing serenely down on the road traffic as their vessel sails slowly past.

Among the multifarious cargoes handled at Birkenhead Docks for many years were locomotives and rolling stock destined for many parts of the World. These were mainly loaded at Cavendish Wharf on the West Float, tracks of different gauges being provided on which they could stand while awaiting shipment. Mostly the locomotives travelled by road transport to the docks from inland manufacturing centres. Passenger coaches and wagons were also loaded at Birkenhead in addition to components such as wheels and bogies etc. During 1942-3 a large number of American-built 2-8-0 locomotives for war service were off-loaded at Cavendish Wharf and hauled to the locomotive depot at Mollington Street, Birkenhead, for preparation before being set to work on British railways, or hauled away to storage dumps awaiting D-Day, after which they would be shipped away over to the Continent.

Grain is one of the most important traffics handled at Birkenhead, as the numerous silos and mills testify, but there was also a multiplicity of general cargoes dealt with. One most notable difference between Birkenhead and Liverpool is the almost complete absence of warehouses at the former. Birkenhead Docks are practically devoid of vast ranges of bonded stores that are such a feature of Liverpool's dockland, except for several railway warehouses. There are many single-storey dockside transit sheds at Birkenhead, however. Many dock buildings were damaged or destroyed during the last war, as Birkenhead Docks were just as important targets as those of Liverpool and Bootle and took a severe hammering from the Luftwaffe.

In 1950 a new rail-served iron-ore berth was completed at Bidston Dock, from which trainloads of ore were hauled to Summers steelworks at Shotton. Vittoria Dock was lengthened in 1960 and a vast new transit shed was opened in 1965, this too being rail-served from the "main line" on Corporation Road.

Since the early 1960's railway traffic on Birkenhead Docks has shown a steady decline and one by one the goods stations have been closed. Seacombe depot at Kelvin Road actually closed in the late 1950's, followed by Shore Road in 1961. The South Reserve with its once busy sidings was also abandoned, and has become an overgrown wilderness with all of its numerous rails removed for scrap. Morpeth Dock depot was closed in October, 1972. In 1975 most of the docks railway system was abandoned, and today most of the vast network of rails that covers the estate is idle with hardly a railway wagon in sight in areas where there once were hundreds of such vehicles. Rubber-tyred vehicles now bounce over rails upon which thousands of steel wheels once clattered, serving small firms which have been established on the docks. Indeed, if anybody who was familiar with Birkenhead dock estate in the 1950's and having been away since then was to make a return visit, the dearth of ships and railway wagons and the absence of the once numerous locomotives would be a source of wonderment.

Not only were trip and shunting movements carried out on the dock railway lines, but long-distance express freight-trains ran to and from the docks, hauled by main-line locomotives which were quite a sight in the streets. There are no such trains nowadays, the late 1960's seeing the last of them.

The "main lines" along Corporation Road, Beaufort Road and Duke Street are the only sections of the dock rail system in use, chiefly for grain traffic to warehouses that have replaced the mills at the West end of Dock Road, which brings the modern "Polybulk" bogie grain wagons onto the estate in place of the older small-capacity grain wagons. Large bogie "Cargowagons" are also used in connection with this traffic. Although there is still some cargo dealt with at Vittoria Dock, only a small amount of it is transported by rail.

One development with a promising future was the establishment of a rail-served steel depot on land that was formerly the yard of the former Cheshire Lines goods depot in Canning Street. Rails were removed from this yard in the late 1960's, but in 1975 a single-line branch was laid from the Egerton Dock line near Canning Street to serve the steel depot. Regrettably however, rail traffic here was of short duration. The branch still survived in 1988, out of use, but there is a scrap metal yard nearby which is rail-served, at the Tower Road · end of the branch.

A coal concentration depot was established at Birkenhead North in 1965, on the site of the old steam locomotive sheds. This replaced most of the local railway coal yards in Wirral, but traffic here has gradually declined. Today it is the National Fuel Distributors depot and still receives some of its coal by rail.

Importing of coal from Australia and elsewhere has taken place from time to time, most being carried by rail to power stations, but early in 1988 imported coal was being transported away by road vehicles, even though rail facilities were still available. The coal is usually unloaded at Duke Street wharf, at which coal tips were once busy, year in and year out. Iron-ore traffic replaced the coal here after the end of World War II, Bidston Dock became the unloading point for John Summers iron-ore in 1950.

Unfortunately, steel-making at the vast. John Summers works at Shotton ceased in February. 1980 and thus the iron ore traffic from Bidston Dock came to an end. Today Bidston Dock is occasionally used for solid bulk traffic conveyed in road vehicles, and is also used for harbouring laid-up ships. Its only occupant early in 1988 was the Isle of Man steamer "Ben-My-Chree" which had spent three years awaiting sale. In the heyday of the Liverpool-Isle of Man service up to half-a-dozen ships were laid up for the Winter in Birkenhead Docks.

Nowadays the only regular traffics at Birkenhead are bulk oils, chemicals and grain. The grain is unloaded at Rea's wharf at Duke Street, but is carried to the mills by road transport. Rails are still in position on the quays so access by rail is still possible. The double track "main line" along Dock Road was relaid with heavy flat-bottom rails during the 1950's. Sections of the inside track have recently been removed however. The only section of this line in use in 1988 was that west of Duke Street as a headshunt and run-round for locomotives. Although the line continues onwards towards Seacombe, partially landscaped on the roadway side and ballasted with white stone chippings, it is unused, and has been cut off from the lines along Tower Road which it once joined and there is now no connection between the latter throughfare and Duke Street via Dock Road. Remnants of branches and sidings abound along Dock Road.

Demolition of the huge mills and warehouses that formerly stood on the north side of Dock Road at the Seacombe end has eliminated the canyon-like aspect of the scene, their replacement by smaller modern buildings now giving a more spacious and open area.

A great deal of track has been removed from Birkenhead and Wallasey Docks in recent times, eliminating some complex junctions, whilst the docks themselves present a scene of desolation with grass, weeds and bushes growing over once busy dockland sites, something hardly imaginable 20 years ago. Only Vittoria Dock, Cavendish and Duke Street Wharves and Bidston Dock are the main cargo handling locations today, but ships can still be seen tied-up elsewhere. The oil and molasses depots at the west end of the estate are still busy, but served by road transport even though they still have rails on their premises. Quite a lot of landscaping with grass verges, trees and white stone chippings has been carried out along the full length of Dock Road on its south side, but this only serves to emphasise the decline of the area for sea and rail traffic.

Over recent years road repairs have created gaps in various parts of the rail network that still survives, though abandoned, whilst some lines have had small industrial buildings erected on them. The curves leading from the junction at Canning Street into Tower Road have had an ornamental garden made over them! At the west end of the docks, the double track curves from Beaufort Road to the oil depot and other premises along Wallasey Bridge Road now end abruptly at a raised kerb, and has been landscaped with nice white ballast and grass verges! No track remains on Wallasey Bridge Road, Bidston Dock now being served from the BR Wirral line, and by one line of the former double track along Dock Road. The Bidston Moss Refuse Destructor stands on the site of former railway sidings and odd lengths of rail can be discerned on the west verges of Wallasey Bridge Road.

The Merseyside Development Corporation has taken over the area bounded by Shore Road, Tower Road and the south side of Alfred Dock for leisure and residential development, the filling-in of Morpeth, Egerton and Wallasey Docks being included in the scheme. Work on re-surfacing Tower Road, burying all the rails commenced in the Spring of 1988, and demolition of transit sheds was also put in hand. The Alfred Dock locks will provide the only access from the Mersey for ships using the remainder of the dock system, which is by no means dead, and perhaps the Channel Tunnel scheme might bring increased business, as merchandise could be unloaded at Birkenhead and taken by rail at high speed direct to the Continent. Time alone will tell, and those rusty rails might shine once again with frequent passage of steel wheels

B.R. Class 03 Diesel shunter 03170 hauling grain hoppers along Beaufort Road, Birkenhead Docks in 1984.   Photo — R.L. Wilson

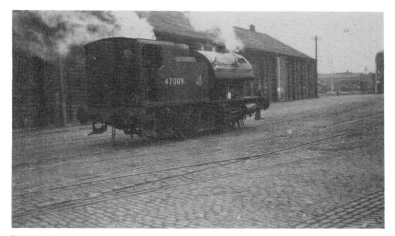

British Railways 0-4-0 Saddle Tank No. 47009 on Birkenhead Docks in 1957.
Photo E.V. Richards

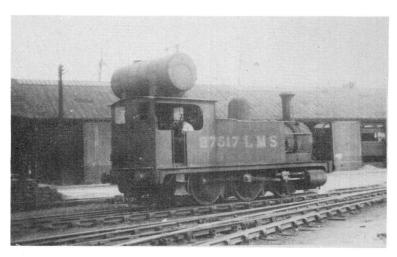

LMS No. 27517, a former North London Railway 0-6-0 Tank engine at Birkenhead Docks in 1947. Note the water tank made from an old boiler (it is not on top of the engine!)
Photo — N.N. Forbes

No. 41853 in its new B.R. guise at Birkenhead Docks in 1949. This 0-6-0 Tank engine was built by the former Midland Railway Co. Photo — E.V. Richards

East African Railways & Harbour Board 2-8-4 locomotive No. 3146. Built by the Vulcan Foundry and awaiting shipment at Birkenhead in 1954.
Photo — G.W. Rose

Three of Reas Diesel shunters on Birkenhead Docks, 1980.
Photo — R.L. Wilson

British Railways ex-North London Railway 0-6-0 Tank engine No. 58857 (ex-LMS 27517) at work on Birkenhead Docks in June, 1951. Photo A. Fisher

CHAPTER SIX

Engines in Great Variety

For anyone interested in locomotives, Birkenhead Docks was, until quite recently, an absolute paradise. The London & North Western, Great Western, Great Central and Wirral systems served the area, therefore a considerable variety of locomotives were at work, especially after the Grouping when engines from other districts and other railways were transferred. Taking firstly the London Midland & Scottish, which absorbed the L&NW and Wirral systems, the native L&NW 0-6-0 Special Saddle Tank and 0-4-2 Bissell Truck engines were partially replaced by 0-6-0 Tank engines from the North Staffordshire and Midland systems, whilst some Lancashire & Yorkshire 0-6-0 Saddle Tank engines also made their way to Birkenhead. The strangest migration of all was that of several 0-6-0 Tank engines from the North London Railway, which were sent to work at Birkenhead and proved to be reliable and popular. Two LMS Standard designs of shunting engine also appeared on Birkenhead Docks, the 3F 0-6-0 Side Tank, and smaller 0-6-0 Dock Tank with a short wheelbase. After the formation of British Railways several 0-4-0 Saddle Tank engines, modifications of an earlier Kitson/LMS design were sent to Birkenhead. Main-line locomotives of a large variety of types visited the docks with incoming freight trains or to take out trains which had been made-up by the regular shunting locomotives.

The Great Western was represented, so far as shunting is concerned solely by its characteristic 0-6-0 Pannier Tank engines of various classes and vintages. Some of them had a bell mounted on top of the boiler, as also did some L&NWR engines, but there were no motion-worked continuously tolling bells fitted, as were required in Liverpool. Some of the older GWR engines had open cabs which gave scant weather protection to the crew but gave a clear view in busy traffic areas. Main-line Great Western engines brought trains in and out of the docks, such as 2-8-0's of the 28XX and 38XX and 47XX classes, along with "Hall" and "Grange" class 4-6-0's. The versatile 43XX 2-6-0's were also regularly used.

The London & North Eastern Railway absorbed the Great Central, and therefore had a share in the Birkenhead Docks traffic and, like the LMS brought engines in from far afield. For dock shunting the Great Central used small 0-6-0 Saddle and Side Tank engines which became LNER Classes J.61 and J.62 respectively. Large LNER engines seldom ventured onto the dock estate, trains from and to distant places being hauled to and from Bidston sidings by the shunters. Many main-line locomotive classes visited the nearby Bidston depot, itself only having small engines allocated until BR days.

After the 1923 Grouping, 0-6-0 Tank engines from the North Eastern Railway (LNER Class J.72) and the Great Eastern Railway (LNER Class J.69) were brought to Bidston for dock area work, and after World War 2 some ex-War Department 0-6-0 Saddle Tank engines (Class J.94) arrived.

After the formation of British Railways in 1948 things remained as they were for a while, but BR standard locomotive types appeared, and later on various main-line diesel-electric machines appeared along Duke Street and Beaufort Road. In 1956 most of the dock shunting was taken over by diesel locomotives, the first arrivals being Hudswell-Clarke (Leeds) 0-6-0's of the series D2500-2519. Other shunters came later, the 0-6-0 diesel-electric now Class 08 appeared. Today this class is still employed, as also are the small, neat 0-6-0 diesels, BR Class 03. There is not much work for them nowadays, alas.

Post-war iron ore traffic at Bidston Dock was handled by a small fleet of diesel shunting engines owned by Reas until the closure of John Summers steel works at Shotton. Haulage of the iron ore trains between Bidston and Shotton was performed by ex-LMS Class 8F 2-8-0's and occasionally by ex-Great Central 2-8-0's of Class 04. Latterly the BR Standard Class 9F 2-10-0's were put on this work, the largest locomotives ever to be seen at Bidston. In 1967 diesel-electric locomotives of Classes 25 and 47 took over the iron ore workings until they ceased in February 1980.

Although the Mersey Docks & Harbour Board owned most of the railway lines on Birkenhead and Wallasey Docks, they only provided part of the locomotive power, with transfers of engines to and from Liverpool from time to time. They ceased haulage on this side of the Mersey in 1932. The MD&HB used two large Avonside 0-6-0 Saddle Tank engines, No's 3 and 4 on Bidston Dock construction, after which they were transferred to Liverpool for general haulage, in December, 1932. After that year all dock haulage in Birkenhead, apart from that by the main-line railway companies was carried out by contractors.

As mentioned previously, Messers T.R & J.J Nickson were permitted to use their own locomotive on the dock lines in 1882. In the same year the Mersey Railway Company were permitted to use a locomotive for hauling spoil from their tunnel works, and also bricks from Morpeth dock to the work site.

In 1887 Messers Meakin & Dean were allowed to use a locomotive for hauling sand and ashes from E.Logan's yard on the West Float to Wallasey Bridge Road station of the Seacombe, Hoylake & Deeside Railway. The latter took over the haulage in 1890.

The English McKenna Process Company, the previously mentioned steel works which was at Gorsey Lane/Duke Street from 1903 until 1911, had an 0-4-0 Saddle Tank engine built by Hudswell Clarke in 1904.

Apart from regularly employed engines on the docks, various civil engineering works saw temporary lines laid, some of narrow gauge on which locomotives were used for hauling materials and spoil, and which departed upon completion of the projects.

Over the years various firms and haulage contractors on the dock estate had a wonderful variety of locomotives, most of them being short wheelbase 0-4-0 Saddle Tanks. It is not possible to deal here with every individual locomotive that has worked on Birkenhead docks, because the subject is very complex and gaps still exist in the available information. However taking say, the year 1946, the locomotive historian was delighted by such outstandingly interesting engines as "Avon", an inside cylinder 0-6-0 Saddle Tank operated by Joseph Perrin & Son Ltd. This specimen which had an archaic high arched fire box and domeless boiler was built by Manning Wardle, Leeds, in 1887. There was widespread regret when "Avon" was broken up in 1950, for it was possibly the last working locomotive in the country with a fire box of the kind concerned.

Another old Birkenhead stalwart was "Cyclops", an 0-4-0 Saddle Tank with outside cylinders, built by Hudswell Clark & Co Ltd., of Leeds in 1895. This battle-scarred veteran was also in the employ of Joseph Perrin & Son Ltd. and led a hard life. By 1947 it was decrepit in looks but not in condition, for it hauled prodigious loads, often causing lorry drivers to widen eyes in astonishment when they passed the little engine along the street with a lengthy train behind it. "Cyclops" was fitted with a melodious chime whistle. It was scrapped alas, in 1964, having become one of the last steam locomotives to remain at work in Birkenhead docks.

The most resplendent engine in Birkenhead was "Homepride", an 0-4-0 Saddle Tank with outside cylinders owned by Messrs. Paul Bros, flour millers, and built by Hawthorn Leslie & Co., Newcastle-on-tyne, in 1924. "Homepride" was a joy to behold in its bright red livery with plenty of polished brasswork. It ceased to be used at the flour mill in 1958 and was then operated by W.J. Lee until 1964. Unfortunately "Homepride" was scrapped at Birkenhead in the latter year.

An engine that caused much puzzlement because of its odd number, was B17C. It was an 0-4-0 Saddle Tank with outside cylinders, similar to "Homepride" just described and from the same builder, but much older, having been completed in 1900. It was latterly used by Rea Ltd., and worked until 1960. The engine had formerly been owned by the Butterley Company.

Another very old engine which was at Birkenhead Docks, for many years was "Shamrock", an 0-4-0 Saddle Tank built by the Hunslet Engine Company of Leeds, in 1886, and subsequently rebuilt by Cudworth & Johnston of Wrexham ,who owned it, but hired it to W.J. Lee. "Shamrock", appropriately painted green, was sent on loan in 1955 to Wm. Crawford & Sons biscuit factory in Binns Road, Liverpool while that establishment's own engine was being overhauled, but returned to Birkenhead and put in a further five years service, largely at Duke Street Wharf, until replaced by diesel in 1960.

In great contrast to the veterans already mentioned there was "Kelvinside" owned by Messrs. Currie & Rowlands of Seacombe. This was an 0-4-0 Saddle Tank built in 1947 by Hudswell Clarke of Leeds, but worked only for a few years, being laid-up in 1961 and scrapped in 1965.

One of the quaintest engines on Birkenhead Docks was "Sulphur". An 0-4-0 Saddle Tank with outside cylinders, built by Robert Stephenson & Hawthorns Ltd. It belonged to the Britannia Scrap Metal Co. Ltd., Widnes and was loaned to Joseph Perrin & Son Ltd., in 1952. With its dumpy form and open-back cab it put one in mind of a child's wooden toy engine!

The aforementioned are just a few of the many locomotives that have worked on Birkenhead docks. With the general decline of rail traffic private steam locomotivees were not replaced by diesel machines, except at Duke Street Wharf when steam engines on the iron ore shunting were supplanted by internal combustion locomotives in 1960. A sad line of idle steam locomotives was to be seen in Duke Street in the latter year as they stood awaiting disposal, rusting and forlorn, after years of hard, reliable service.

Steam returned briefly to Birkenhead Docks in July, 1972 when the Liverpool Locomotive Preservation Group, which has two industrial locomotives — a Barclay 0-4-0 Saddle Tank named "Efficient" and an Avonside 0-6-0 Saddle Tank named "Lucy", used both to haul a train of BR goods brake vans in which rode local railway enthusiasts. Needless to say the train created plenty of interest as it visited various parts of the dock estate over practically deserted tracks. The Society kept the two locomotives in the small engine shed at the end of Birkenhead Road near its junction with Dock Road, but in 1973 road works caused removal of the rails in the street, thus isolating the shed from the railway system. Both locomotives were removed to the transport museum that has been established at the former locomotive depot in Southport. "Lucy" made a return visit to the docks in 1978, being brought by road transport to haul a special train for railway enthusiasts. No more steam specials have been run on the dock estate since, but Beaufort Road has been traversed by several diesel hauled enthusiasts trains formed of passenger coaches, whilst diesel multiple-unit trains, also for entusiasts have passed along that road causing astonishment among the residents of the district.

There was a great variety of names carried by the industrial locomotives on Birkenhead docks. Some were names of local interest or personalities, others bore names or the products or brand names of the firms which owned them, whilst some engines obtained second hand kept the names they arrived at Birkenhead with. Undoubtedly the engine with the most beautiful name was "Silver Queen", an 0-4-0 Saddle Tank built by the Hunslet Engine Company, Leeds in 1879. This engine was owned by Buchanan's the flour millers at Seacombe.

There is no doubt that the industrial steam locomotive was a tough machine and capable of many years of hard slog and even abuse. The great age of many of the locomotives on Birkenhead Docks is ample proof of this fact. Its successors, the diesels, whilst having greater availability, cannot be abused in the same way, being precision machines needing perfect maintenance, whilst the steam engine was simple and rugged and could keep going even in a battered and dilapidated state.

"Cyclops" operated on Birkenhead Docks by W.J. Lee & Co. Built by Hudswell Clarke, Leeds in 1895. Seen here on Dock Road, Seacombe in August, 1955.
Photo J.F. Ward

J. Perrin & Sons locomotive "Walter Scott", built by Manning Wardle, Leeds in 1891. Derelict at Shore Road, Birkenhead in May, 1950.
Photo — K.J. Cooper

J. Perrin & Sons locomotive "Avon", built by Manning Wardle, Leeds in 1887. Photographed at Shore Road, Birkenhead in May, 1950.
Photo — K.J. Cooper

"Shamrock", operated on Birkenhead Docks by W.J. Lee & Co. Built by the Hunslet Engine Co., Leeds in 1886. Photographed in August, 1959.
Photo — J.A. Peden

CHAPTER SIX (Part Two)

Rolling Stock

Although passenger coaches did not normaly grace the rails of Birkenhead Docks except vehicles being exported, there were many superannuated carriages shorn of their wheels and used as mess rooms, huts and offices. At Canning Street North there were several examples, including an 1890's period L&NWR corridor coach and a former London Metropolitan Railway vehicle. Sadly, in 1985 Cavendish sidings were the graveyard of many 1938 Wirral electric trains that had been replaced by the new class 507/8 units, and after they had been scrapped, some of the sidings were removed.

Goods wagons were of course, in great variety — wagons from all the main line railways and privately owned coal wagons for domestic and export coal. The Acme Coal & Firelighter Company of Corporation Road had their own wagons whilst Spillers Ltd., employed a number of ex-Midland Railway vans at Seacombe Mills until the late 1950's, when they were replaced by ex-Lancashire & Yorkshire Railway vans. These however vanished in 1960. They were used internally on Dock Road for haulage between mills and did not go out on the main lines.

The end of the line for "Melsonby", built in 1906 by Manning Wardle of Leeds, standing derelict at Seacombe in 1955.   Photo — J.F. Ward

By the late 1980's the long traditional small-capacity four-wheeled goods wagons had almost vanished from revenue-earning service, having been replaced by high-capacity bogie vehicles for bulk loads, whilst a new generation of high-capacity four-wheeled vans and wagons form the "Speedlink" fleet for individual wagon loads. Upon Nationalisation in 1948, one and a quarter million wagons passed into the ownership of British Railways, but only a fraction of that immense total forms the wagon fleet today. Indeed, a freight train is a comparatively rare sight these days, but this may change when road traffic reaches saturation point. Whatever happens though, the vast variety of wagons used in former times will never be seen again.

POST SCRIPT 1991

Since completion of the manuscript in 1989 alterations and developments along the line of docks have continued, so in order to bring the story up to date (mid-1991) the following notes must be added.

North Docks

Gladstone Dock has become the unloading point for imported coal, and this traffic has reached such an extent that the railway between Alexandra Dock and Edge Hill has been completely re-laid with heavy welded rail in order that trains conveying 1,000 tons can be operated day and night. The coal is taken to the power station at Fiddlers Ferry. Increased traffic in containers has also meant greater use of the line.

The great corn warehouse at East Waterloo Dock has been converted into living accommodation and all railway track in the vicinity has been removed. Messrs. Bibby's great complex of works and warehouses has been demolished and the firm has new premises at Canada Dock.

Riverside station, long isolated from the railway system was demolished in 1990. A proposal was made for its use as a transport museum, but this came to nought.

Stanley Dock warehouse is used as a leisure and market site and is destined to remain, along with the adjacent hydraulic tower. Some railway track survives here. The future of the great Stanley Tobacco warehouse is in doubt however.

South Docks

Former Great Western Railway dock sheds at Mann Island once associated with Manchester Dock have been restored and new Great Western signs affixed. An office building of the London & North Western Railway on the same site has been demolished. Some old dock cottages in Irwell Street have been demolished, amid much protest, and the site is now occupied by an ugly car showroom which upsets the old-world scene in this quarter.

On Canning Dock north quay reposed the original railway track which was laid in 1866 and consisted of iron rails and points of the earliest kind used on the docks railway system, probably the last surviving examples. These, and the cobblestones on the quay were removed early in 1990 and the quay re-paved, used now for parking cars. It is sad that, in a so-called heritage area such artifacts should be discarded. Not only was the quay picturesque in its own way, but the rails were of technical interest as well as being the last vestige of the docks railway in the vicinity.

The great Wapping warehouse has fortunately been retained and converted into apartments at high prices. The hydraulic tower at its south end has also been retained and restored. All has not been lost here so far as the railway is concerned, as a few yards of double track have been left in place where the line entered Queen's Dock, and trees planted between the rails! A new hotel now stands on the site of the old transit sheds on the dock road side of the dock.

At Coburg Dock the two great grain silos have been demolished (1989) and a vast open space exists where they once reared their gigantic bulk. All the complex railway track here remains, but partially buried under gravel and rubble.

Most of the old industrial buildings on the east side of the dock road between Parliament Street and Hill Street remain, including the former Great Western Railway depot at Norfolk Street which has been cleaned and refurbished but untennanted. Many of the buildings are to let, however. The sites of the former L&Y and L&NWR goods depots on Sefton Street were still empty in July 1991, but the Cheshire lines yard site is now occupied by small industrial buildings.

Birkenhead Dock area

Great changes are in progress in the area of Woodside, Shore Road and Tower Road. All railway track has been removed from the roadways (or covered over) and only the main line from Grange Road, along Corporation Road and Beaufort Road remain in use, along with a few sidings. Housing and small industrial development is taking place over an area formerly occupied by Egerton, Morpeth and Wallasey Docks which have been, or will be filled-in. Elsewhere part industry and part desolation remain, Alfred Dock being the only one to remain of the docks at the riverward end. Vittoria Dock still sees some use, but the Blue-Funnel line terminal, built in the 1960's is long derelict.

A "museum" tramway is to be constructed on Shore Road, with a warehouse on Pacific Quay, Morpeth Dock, to be used as a tram shed. A transport museum is also to be made in the Shore Road area. Little progress had been made by mid-1991 however.

119